Goetia Pathworking

Magickal Results from The 72 Demons

Corwin Hargrove

All Rights Reserved. This book may not be copied, reproduced, in whole or in part, in any form or by any means electronic or mechanical, or by any method now known or hereafter invented, without written permission from Corwin Hargrove.

All images in this book are subject to copyright. Where traditional sources have been used, they have been crafted into entirely new images, and may not be copied or shared, commercially or gratis.

Disclaimer: The content of this book is based on personal experience and conjecture and should be regarded as speculative entertainment and not professional, medical, financial, or personal advice. The concepts and practices presented here are to be used at your own risk. Corwin Hargrove is not responsible for the experiences you obtain from working with the methods presented. It is hereby stated clearly and in full that the author neither suggests nor condones that you ever act in a way that can cause harm, and this book is provided with the understanding that the materials be used in accordance with the laws of your country or any country in which you are present.

Copyright © 2019 Corwin Hargrove

TABLE of CONTENTS

Pathworking the Goetia	9
Pathworking Keys	11
The Work of Magick	13
The Desired Result	21
Elemental Pathworking	27
Before the Magick	31
The Pathworking Method	35
Pathworking The 72 Demons	41
1. Bael	44
2. Agares	46
3. Vassago	48
4. Gamigin	50
5. Marbas	52
6. Valefar	54
7. Amon	56
8. Barbatos	58
9. Paimon	60
10. Buer	62
11. Gusoin	64
12. Sitri	66
13. Beleth	68
14. Leraye	70
15. Eligos	72
16. Zepar	74
17. Botis	76
18. Bathin	78

19. Sallos	80
20. Purson	82
21. Marax	84
22. Ipos	86
23. Aim	88
24. Naberius	90
25. Glasya Labolas	92
26. Bime	94
27. Ronove	100
28. Berith	102
29. Astaroth	104
30. Forneus	106
31. Foras	108
32. Asmodai	110
33. Gaap	112
34. Furfur	114
35. Marchosias	116
36. Stolas	118
37. Phenix	120
38. Halphas	122
39. Malphas	124
40. Raum	126
41. Forcalor	128
42. Vepar	130
43. Sabnock	132
44. Shax	134
45. Vine	136
46. Bifrons	138
47. Vuall	140
48. Haagenti	142
49. Crocell	144
50. Furcas	146
51. Balam	148
52. Alloces	150
53. Caim	152
54. Murmus	154
55. Orobas	156

56. Gremori	158
57. Oso	160
58. Auns	162
59. Orias	164
60. Vapula	166
61. Zagan	168
62. Valac	170
63. Andras	172
64. Haures	174
65. Andrealphus	176
66. Cimeries	178
67. Amducias	180
68. Belial	182
69. Decarabia	184
70. Seer	186
71. Dantalion	188
72. Andromalius	190
Questions and Answers	193
Alternative Names	201
Unbibliography	205

Pathworking the *Goetia*

Magick is easier and safer than many people believe, and pathworking is a method that takes you to the essence of power.

There are many ways of working with demons. The spirits of *Goetia* can bring knowledge, manipulate reality, produce changes within yourself, or attract conditions and events that you desire. This is widely known. Demons are famed for their speed, dignity, and willingness to cooperate with you.

What is less well known is that incredibly simple pathworking rituals enable you to make easy contact with these demons, safely and reliably.

Advantages of The Pathworking Method

- No difficult words of power to learn or speak.

- Nothing to burn, collect, or make.

- No sacrifice, reward, or offering is required.

- No sigils need to be drawn, and you only need to look at the sigils in this book.

- No angels or divine names are used, which makes the magick feel more reliable for some people.

- The method automatically creates the correct state of mind and summons elemental energy.

- Pathworking can be performed in complete privacy.

- The method is extremely safe and easy to learn.

Pathworking is an undertaking of imagination, but you don't need special skills. If you have a desire, *that* is imagination.

Anything you *want* that you *don't* yet have - *that's* your imagination telling you what you want.

You will never have to learn difficult visualisation methods or train in demanding mental techniques.

These pathworkings are useful when you are looking for a way to make a request to a demon. You ask for something, and you get it, without any repercussion or payment.

Some people say you never get something for nothing. Here, you get something because you've performed magick and filled it with your desire. That is enough.

In pathworking, images are used to align you with the spirit you're trying to contact. For *Goetia* pathworking, you will use Elemental Imagery. Although I'll explain what this means, all you need to know for now is that the magick is as easy as picturing a sequence of images and then communicating your desire to the demon.

Even if you think you can't imagine, this method works. If you see the word 'tree', you know what a tree is. That degree of imagination is all you need, combined with the inner imagination of desire.

Pathworking creates a correspondence of desire, where your desire becomes the demon's desire. That is why it works and why it's safe. With the correspondence of desire, there's no need for the authority of angels and no need for a reward or sacrifice of any kind. Getting the result is what the demon wants too, when you use this method.

The spirits of *Goetia* are thought of as demons, and they have a quality of power that is different from angels, but I don't want you to get hung up on the idea that demons are evil, reckless, careless, and debased, as many believe.

The word demon comes from a Greek word which used to mean 'spirit'. If you call these spirits demons, what do *you* mean by demon? Do you believe these labels have anything to do with good and evil? I use the word demon for the *Goetia* spirits because to me the word does not mean there is evil, only that there is change. There is change that comes through power and wisdom. How you choose to use the power determines whether you do good or evil more than the nature of the demons themselves.

These seventy-two demon spirits are more obedient than many spirits, more willing to help, and will deal out wisdom and change that can last a long time. There's a belief that demons work fast and dirty, while angels work to bring the highest good that they can. I don't agree. The results can be fast, but they are not haphazard or short-lived. Believe what you want, but for me, I work with the powers and see what I can get out of this.

If you want to know the history of the demons you can scout around online (it's unreliable information, but at least it's some information) or you can read books like Peterson's *The Lesser Key of Solomon*, but to *really* learn about demons, *use* their magick.

Your knowledge, after one ritual, will be greater than that of any professor of occultism. As I said in another book, when you read too much about demons you get confused, upset, opinionated, bored, and dispirited. I say you should try the magick instead. It's good stuff, and it doesn't need to be complicated.

If you think there's a higher purpose to magick (and I do), then you'll be led there by the results you get and the magickal path that appears before you. But this is a book written to help you get results from the *Goetia* demons, and that's all you need to get started.

Pathworking Keys

Things have changed in the past few years, with secret methods now being published freely and often. Many readers have no idea they are accessing centuries of experience that's been condensed into the simplest magickal formulas.

In some systems, the magick is almost as easy as saying a few words. But I don't want you to think it's all so simple that it's basic. It's simple because it contains the essence of the complex understanding of many occultists. Simplicity doesn't mean stupidity.

I wrote a book on influence, which people liked, and it included a few *Goetia* demons. In that book they were summoned more traditionally, using divine names, angelic powers, circles of protection, rewards, and spoken requests. That method does work, and I'll talk about it later, but in this book, you get a pure method that enables you to connect with all the demons' powers.

Some readers asked me to write a book about *Goetia* using the method from the influence book, but I believe *this* will be more useful. (If you really want to use the method from the earlier book, I explain how you can at the end.)

I considered saving this book for another time, because it's now early 2019, and pathworking is fashionable. I'm not here to follow trends, but I don't feel the need to be revolutionary, so I decided I would stick to my plan. This is the next book I wanted to write, and here it is, whatever anybody else is doing. I write the books of practical magick that I believe will be useful to you.

Some writers push the idea that you can make up your own pathworking for a demon. I agree with them, but it's not as easy as it sounds. If you are skilled enough to use evocation to contact demons, you can then build a pathworking by asking the demon to provide one for you. After years of evoking a demon, that is sometimes how you work with that demon. But like I said, evocation is difficult. You can skip all that and use this book instead.

A personal pathworking is usually only useful to you, but some pathworkings are universal, and that's what you need for a book like this. Discovering them is not easy. Using evocation, you ask the demons to reveal the universal pathworkings. It takes many years to discover the precise pathworkings that can work for other people. There is no single solution, and I have seen other pathworkings (even though they were given another name) that work, but I am revealing the ones that I believe to be the best.

The pathworkings in this book are not all my own but have been crafted by many occultists. They can work for anybody willing to use the magick and methods described in this book.

I have even shown beginners how to use this method, and they got results. If you're a beginner, the pathworkings can work for you. If you've already used *Goetia* with success, you might enjoy this method as a form of shortcut, or a way of extending your abilities.

I write about getting results, but all that talk about evocation might have made you want to summon a demon to make contact through evocation (where you see and hear the demon). If so, there are many methods published elsewhere, and none are easy. Maybe I can satisfy your curiosity by telling that with pathworking you get a feeling that's similar to evocation, without the difficult rituals. This is known as The Summoned Presence.

During the pathworking you are with the demon, the demon is with you, and you will sense this reality. You might not sense it the first time you do magick, especially if you're afraid or closed off to the energies, but if you are sensitive, you will soon feel how real and powerful this magick can be through The Summoned Presence.

Pathworking makes this form of contact easy because you are not *aiming* to see and hear the demon. You are only aiming to be *understood* by the demon, and that means you let go of the fanatical urgency to see a demon. Full evocation has its place in magick, but the simplified method of pathworking will get you what you want, and I think for most people, that's what matters. Sensing the demon is an interesting side-effect that will happen sometimes.

If you've never performed any magick, or if you've never worked with demons, this might sound terrifying. Full evocation can be frightening at first, but this magick is not evocation and is not going to scare you. When you sense the presence of a demon through The Summoned Presence, it's unusual, but what you feel is more about awe and excitement than it is about fear. You remain in control.

Sensing a demon may take time, but it doesn't matter, because even if you feel nothing at all, the magick works.

The Work of Magick

Magick is incredibly rewarding. It doesn't work 100% of the time, but neither does a dishwasher. If you think magick should work every time, let me mention the dangers of entitlement. You should expect results but don't go into a sulk when something doesn't work first time. A small failure is usually a step to a bigger success. If you don't panic.

I keep away from online occult groups and forums, and even tell readers to be careful not to spend too much time there because you get more out of doing magick than talking about it. But somebody told me to have a look recently, and I had to admit there was some interesting work in one or two groups. But the bad stuff was worse than I thought. Would-be gurus making stupid claims about their powers is now the least of the problems. The real problem is the prevalence of laziness. You see people saying, 'I can't be arsed doing the first part of the ritual. Does it matter?' There are many similar complaints that magick is too difficult. These people have no idea how easy it's all become.

Imagine that you're in a dark place, with a demon standing before you, completely real, and you can feel its icy breath, the stench of its wet flesh, and the glittering power in its eyes. Imagine this towering demon, looking down at you. Can you imagine looking back and whining, 'Hey Sitri, I want to get laid but can't be arsed doing the whole ritual. Does it matter?'

It wouldn't happen. In the presence of a demon, most people are stunned and fumble into pathetic levels of respect. The mask of the brave and bold occultist is quickly shattered by that kind of experience. That won't happen with this magick (you can relax!) because there is no evocation, but you should consider this imagery, and remember that you are not saying a few magick words to nothingness. You are saying them *to a demon*, and you should believe that demon is a real entity. When you do that, entitlement fades away, and that is good.

Magick should feel important, astonishing, and powerful, not like a crazy favour you're owed by a glorified pixie.

I am tired of seeing a level of entitlement where people assume that magick should bring instant rewards or else they will declare all magick a failure. Magick fails, but people fail their magick far more frequently, by being lazy or unfocused.

If you doubt me, commit to doing this as well as you can, within the confines of what I suggest is possible. Your confidence and patience will be rewarded far more than an angry demand for the magick to work.

Remember that the demons are real and that you are communicating with them. This doesn't mean you have to be afraid of the demons, but treat them as real entities. It will ground you in the reality of magick.

People who say modern magick is too hard have no idea. Somebody else made an opposing point (in the week when I was completing this book) that this is a golden age for magick. Right through the eighties, nineties, and beyond, you were stuck with old copies of complex texts, with rituals that took months or years. Or you had to join an 'order' and spend a year being initiated. Or maybe you'd track down some books on tarot and witchcraft. That's how it was for most people.

I was fortunate to find people who knew the workings of magick. The lesser-known orders worked recklessly at times, but with a drive to develop magick and make it work, above all else. Now, people who lived through that era are sharing the knowledge.

There were many secrets, hidden completely from the public. Today, a lot of really astonishing, simplified rituals of practical magick have been published. If you like magick, this is a good time to be around. If you think magick is something you can't be arsed with, you're the one deciding to lose.

An entitled attitude is the worst possible attitude you can have when using magick. When you think that magick should give you a result because you're such a luminous entity, you're going to end up being lazy in your intentions, your planning, and your magick. We're talking about a few minutes of easy magick.

Expectation is not the same as entitlement, and you should work on building a sense of expectation. Work on finding a sense of expectation without desperation.

Like most people my age, when I started with *Goetia*, it was all about complexity and drama. Months were spent practicing a banishing, and finding equipment that felt right. I put many hours into building a wooden triangle, scorching in a few words that were meant to constrain the demons. Then I had to find somewhere to draw a complex circle on the floor, hidden from everybody. It was such a great way to waste time. You could spend months getting that ready without doing any magick. Before internet forums came along to help you waste time, occultists wasted their time building stuff they didn't need, and I was guilty of that until I found a better way. Now, people are guilty of reading easy magick books and thinking they're still too hard.

If you can't be arsed to crawl out of bed, don't expect breakfast.

If you think modern magick is too hard, I don't know how you manage to get through the day.

If you're still reading, then you're probably not one of those entitled people, so you'll do well.

Existence owes you nothing, but you can claim everything. When you see what that means, magick becomes easy.

The Desired Result

Your first task is to work out what you want and find the right demon to make your desire become real. I haven't made big lists of Demons for Money or Demons for Love, because those lists are way too limiting. Use lists like that and you miss the good stuff.

When you know what you want, you go through the book and look for a power that looks about right. It doesn't have to be perfect, but you'll know when it's the one you need. Sometimes a power calls to you, and that's a good thing. Sometimes you might see a craftier way to get what you want, and that's good too. It takes longer than having a cheat sheet, but if you use a cheat sheet, you only cheat yourself out of a result. Find out what you want, then go through the book to find a solution. Unless you're very slow, that takes about ten minutes.

But how do you know what you want and what to ask for? The beginner's mistake is usually to aim for everything at once. Magick is so exciting and tempting that you want to slay all your enemies, become a lord of wealth, and get more sex than you have the stamina for. I won't go on about this, but use your common sense.

The demons have immense power, but if you try to change your whole world with one massive desire, or if you try to change everything with fifty half-hearted rituals in one week, not much happens.

At any moment, you can know what you really want by looking at your discomfort. Now imagine how it could change, and that is your desired result. This is the way you get magick to work. Notice what makes you uncomfortable and seek ease.

If you're struggling to pay the bills, easing your discomfort would come from paying the bills and getting out of debt. You don't need to win the lottery for that to happen so don't waste your time on a lottery fantasy. Reality is more rewarding.

That's the only example you need, and you can work out *anything* you need using that logic. Look at your own needs, look at the powers and how they work, and form the idea of a desired result that you want.

What I'm saying here is unoriginal, and you find it in most modern magick books, but that's because it's one of the most important points. You can aim for really big changes with magick, but if you aren't prepared for them, they usually don't happen. Or if they do, they mess you up. I've known people get a big hit of money, and like the stories say, they lose it faster than they got it, because they don't *know* money or how to live with money. But I've known people use magick to *build* a wealthy career, and that gives security and a life of wealth.

When you've worked out your desire, you need to form it into a phrase, so you can pass it on to the demon during the ritual. This is not difficult.

If you look at the power of Buer for *Mental and emotional healing*, your desire might be, 'I want to get over the anxiety of the past month.' You don't need to explain what that means, or what happened last month, because *you* know and that will guide the magick. You don't need to say *how* you will get over the anxiety. You do need to change the phrase, however, so that it is a request.

Some people don't like using requests in magick, and like to say, 'It is my will that...' And some insist that it should be, 'I command that you...' For pathworking, I believe it should be a request, and so you phrase it as, 'I ask that you bring me relief from the anxiety of the past month.'

If you ask, you aren't being hopeful, but opening to the power of cooperation with the demon.

If you are really attached to a different way of working, where you command or impose your will, I suggest you try this method to see what happens. You might prefer it, or you might not. But in pathworking, a request works better than a command or imposed will.

You create a shared desire, so it's like saying to a friend, 'Hey, do you want to go out to dinner?' instead of, 'It is my will that you will eat food!' Demons aren't human, but the point is that requests create the right balance of power and desire.

And, to be unoriginal again, I'll say what everybody else says, because it's true. The less you define *how* the magick should happen, the more likely it is to happen. If you say you want to travel and therefore need a certain amount of money, and support from a partner, and permission from work, and state all these conditions that have to be met, you're making the request too complicated. If you ask for travel, the magick will take care of the details, often in a way you could never have imagined.

Don't try to imagine the *how*. You know what you want and why. The demon will work out how for you. Some people like to add on phrases to qualify the desire, like, 'Without hurting my dog,' or more often, 'Bringing harm to none.' I think these phrases really mess things up because they come from fear, not confidence. And for a demon, they are limiting. Is it possible to do anything in life without bringing harm? When you buy anything in our world, somebody's being exploited somewhere. Focus on what you want, and understand that demons are not the reckless idiots that some people believe. They don't take shortcuts, slaying your family so you can find some extra money. That's movie madness, and it doesn't make sense. The demons know what you want, they know you don't want your family to burn to death to get something you've asked for, so don't add qualifying statements that show you're scared.

In lots of magick books, they say you should make your request in the present tense, like it's already happened. 'I now have all the money I need to pay my debts.' When pathworking, you make a request about the future, and there's no need to pretend it's already worked. The demon works with your lack, your need, with the current reality you *don't* want, and takes the energy of that to empower the change to create or attract what you do want. You make a request for something to change. That example would work better as, 'I ask that you provide all the money I need to pay off my debts.'

This is quite precise, without being *too* precise. It's better to ask for money to pay your debts than to ask for limitless money.

Magick is easy, but you do need to work on developing the skill of knowing what to ask for. You could even leave money out of it and ask to get out of debt, and you might be astonished by the weird coincidences that make it happen.

You don't need to write the phrase down, but you can if it helps you remember, and you will find that magick works best when your request is no more than a short sentence. You won't say the phrase, but you will think it and feel it during the ritual.

Here are some more examples that would work as requests.

The Demon Marbas has the power to *Cast a glamour*, which is a veil of illusion that makes you appear to be something you aren't. If you want to appear as though you are more attractive, because somebody you admire is visiting the city for two weeks, you might phrase it as, 'I ask that you bring an illusion of great beauty to me when in the presence of _____ during her visit.' Why the time limit? You don't have to put a limit on it, but if your intention is to make something happen during those two weeks, the focus might strengthen the result better than if you ask for an ongoing glamour.

The Demon Paimon has the power to *Confuse somebody*, creating a debilitating sense of confusion in one person that you know. If you have a business associate who is causing trouble, and you want him to be incapacitated during the next phase of decision making, you might phrase it as, 'I ask that you fill _____ with extreme confusion.' I wouldn't add a timeframe unless a time limit is relevant to the result. If you know there is a meeting this week, and the magick has to work during this week, say so in your request. You might then phrase it as, 'I ask that you fill _____ with extreme confusion this week.'

The Demon Amducias has the power to *Break the will of another*. If you're going through a divorce and your partner is fighting hard, breaking his will to fight means you'll get what you want, so you might phrase your request as, 'I ask that you break the will of _____ so that he cannot work against me.' In your mind, the timeframe is open, so leave it open in the request.

The Demon Andromalius has the power to *Bring an end to extortion, blackmail, or any threat.* Somebody has found out a secret from your past, and they are threatening to tell people, so you might phrase your request as, 'I ask that _____ never speaks of my secret to anybody.' The demon has the power to bring an end to threats, so you may prefer to phrase the request as, 'I ask that _____ is no threat to me.' Or you could combine the two. You can see from this example that you will gain more satisfaction from the ritual if you put some thought into knowing what result you want.

You can work out this phrasing, and the feeling of your result, hours or days before the ritual, even during the three days of purification, or you can do it in the minutes before you begin the ritual. If you're clear about what you want, any time will be ok.

Elemental Pathworking

The magickal Elements of Earth, Air, Fire, and Water are found throughout magickal practice, and they are reflected symbolically in this book's method of pathworking. For each demon, there are four associated images that are connected to these Elements. These are written beneath the demon's sigil.

The first image you picture is always an image of Earth, which means it is an image of a location, person, or object. The image might be, for example *A black leafless tree in blue moonlight*.

The second image is of Air, and here that means a sound. An example would be *The sound of many feet on gravel.*

The third image is of Water. In these pathworkings, Water is a taste or a scent, such as *The smell of freshly dug soil.*

The final Element is Fire, represented by an image of the sky, often changing from one form to another. You might read *A yellow sky warms to amber as a white sun rises.* You never actually imagine Fire, because the Element of Fire is being represented by light.

By picturing these four Elemental Images in order, with minimal effort, you become present in the awareness of the demon. From that place, you have the power to make your request to the demon, and the demon is compelled by its existence to offer whatever help can be given, according to its powers.

When pathworking with other spirits, such as angels, there can be many combinations of quite complex and striking images. The images used for pathworking the demons are usually much simpler. I have seen pathworkings that involve more complex imagery, but having experimented with those methods, found them to be less powerful than Elemental Imagery.

I think some writers have been so impressed with the images in a recent, popular book on pathworking, which is full of striking images of blood and chains, that there's a bit of a trend now to come up with the best images. I find this concerning because it is essential that the images are genuine keys to the demons being called, rather than images that look impressive.

And I say this because the images in this book are not as striking as you might expect, but that's good news for you. It means it's easier to work with than just about any other pathworking that exists.

By using the demon's sigil, with an awareness of the demon and its powers, and these Elemental Images, you cannot fail but to call the correct demon in a safe way. And in using this approach, the demon will become so aware of you and your needs that you will barely need to make your request. You still make it, obviously, but I think you'll know what I mean when you try this magick. It gives a feeling of peace and ease, so that all you need to do is go into it gently, as instructed, and you will sense that something good will come from your work.

Shouldn't the images all be dramatically different? No. They only need to be true to the demon. You will notice that many images are shared by several demons. The Element of Air is often the sound of *Birdsong*. The Element of Water is often *The taste of charcoal*. You're not looking for variety, but for the pathworking provided by the demons to make contact possible. Enjoy the simplicity.

If you can do that you will almost certainly sense a demon at some point, either through a change in the way the room feels, through noises, glimpses of lights, or tingling down your back. It can happen the first time, or it might not happen for a while, but sensing the demons like this can be reassuring and empowering. If it doesn't happen, don't worry, because the magick works even without any such sensation. But if the sensation comes, enjoy it. The pathworking protects you, and there is no need to pull away from any demonic presence you sense.

This method is the result of the work of many occultists who interpreted the images and sensory impressions given to them by the demons. You may find in other books that to work with a particular demon you must obtain Moonstone Quartz and burn Sandalwood and Cinnamon on a slab of Pyrite. Such approaches are not wrong, but they are systems that have arisen from a vague awareness of the pathworking images, interpreted into concrete forms. You *could* burn cinnamon, but imagining the smell of a rose is enough to get the same effect. You *could* obtain Moonstone Quartz, but picturing a sunset will work. You work through the four Elemental correspondences, and each takes you a step closer to the demon.

Don't worry about getting it wrong. For most people, reading the description is enough to get this right. And if you're already stressing about getting it right, you're already getting it wrong. Doing magick is about performing the magick, not worrying about the details of magick. Try it and see what happens.

You might wonder why there are no descriptions of the demons. What do they look like? According to *The Lesser Key of Solomon*, the demons are described as looking like weird horses, toads, people riding crocodiles, three-headed beasts, and that sort of thing. The old grimoires were often written from personal experience, but it's led to a belief that the demons will look the same to everybody. You can disagree with me, but I believe the demons appear in countless forms. Sometimes they happen to match those old descriptions, but often they don't, and it's still the right demon.

With pathworking, you aren't meant to picture the demon at all, so I'm talking about this to save you the effort of reading up on each demon and trying to picture it as described. Trying to imagine the demon will make the work more difficult. You know the demon through its name, its sigil, by reading about all its powers to get a sense of what 'personality' and power it might have, and then by pathworking your way to the demon. There is no need for more elaborate images. Keep it simple.

In the ritual you breathe out an Elemental Breath onto the sigil, passing the pathworking image into the sigil, to activate a connection to the demon. This is easy to do, but you should understand the concept of Elemental Breath for it to work.

When using this technique, your breath represents the four Elements. Air is obvious because you know that your breath is Air. Water is also obvious because you know your breath contains moisture. For Earth, understand that we are carbon-based beings and our body transfers carbon to every breath we take in before we breathe out. This is like transferring Earth into breath. For Fire, there is obvious warmth in your breath, but also the Fire of your imagination. As you picture the image leaving you and being breathed into the sigil, the Element of Fire is within your breath. When performing the technique, you do not need to think about all this, but I think it helps to know that your breath symbolically holds all the magickal Elements.

Before the Magick

Modern magick gives you ways to jump in, say the magick words, and it's all over before it's started. The problem with that is that the magick can feel too unmagickal. There's not enough weight given to the magick. When your magick feels trivial, the results can be trivial. And yes, I've written books that make it too easy, so I'm not pointing fingers. When readers respect and feel the true power of the magick, it works. If they see it as a silly spell that probably won't work, it never works.

Traditional magick was heavy on the preparation, with months of fasting, prayer, and cleansing. I don't want to make you do that, and there's no need to spend three weeks gathering herbs or building any equipment. There is, however, some work to do before the magick.

Nobody likes to prepare for magick. There's so much easy magick where you can find five minutes and perform a ritual, why should you do anything else? You might be tempted to skip any talk of preparation and get to the rituals. If you do, you'll wonder why the magick didn't work, and you'll blame the magick when it's actually you that couldn't summon up the discipline to prepare. So, here's the truth: I've found that *some* preparation helps the magick to work.

It's pretty easy. You don't have to spend a week in a trance. The only thing you need is to spend some time achieving a degree of purification. The word 'purification' makes it sound like a religious confession, but it's easier than that. The purification I recommend is not about becoming pure in the moral sense, but about removing the dross of thought and distraction, bringing your attention to the magick. This makes you more visible to the demons, so that they are open to your pathworking efforts.

It sounds old-fashioned, but look at it this way; you can't get out of bed, stuff some breakfast down and smoke a cigarette, while sipping your coffee, and expect the great and glorious demons of magick to give a damn about you. Sort yourself out and get in a state that shows some respect for magick. It makes sense.

There is something I should confess before going any further, and that is that many readers told me the purification wasn't needed. They read my other book, the influence book, skipped the purification, and they still got good results. I know that telling you this is a risk because you'll assume that you *can* skip this stage. Maybe you can. I recommend trying it first. If not, try it when magick fails. I accept that the magick may work without the purification, but I still recommended it if you want to do this seriously.

This is my guide to purification. Don't have sex for three days before the ritual, and that includes sex with yourself. Abstaining sharpens your mind and intensifies your will. It's not fun, but it works. How much do you want this magickal result?

If you need to use the magick in an emergency and don't have three days in which to abstain, try to do the magick a few hours after you last had sex. You don't want to get out of bed, sweaty and steaming with satisfaction, and call on the spirits. You'll be too relaxed. It doesn't work well. Abstain for three days if you can, and wait another hour after the magick before you have sex again.

Before the ritual, shower and put on fresh clothes. Some occultists like robes, but I feel like a dick when I see myself in the mirror wearing a robe. Ordinary clothes are best for me.

You can take a bath instead, of course, but I find it a bit too dreamy and relaxing, whereas a shower invigorates. You want to be relaxed but focused, and a sleepy bath might make you too zoned out.

I shower, wash my hair, I put on ordinary fresh clothes, I do the magick, then I take those clothes off after the ritual and put them in the wash, then put my civvies back on.

What if you're at work? What if it's the middle of the night? Ok, showering and changing clothes is ideal, but if you can't do that, at least wash your hands and face. Take off your glasses and your jacket. Make it feel like a purification even if it isn't. Ideally, shower and do the rest, but if not, do what you can.

Skip a meal. I know that's a big ask. Have you seen how many dieting books there are? Thousands. And if any of those books said, 'Skip one meal a day,' you can imagine the shitstorm. Nobody likes to skip a meal. But how much do you want this magick to work? If you want it to work, skip whatever meal might leave you feeling full and satisfied when it comes to ritual time. And skip other comforts such as coffee. You think a cup of coffee wakes you up, but it pacifies you. You want to be wired on yourself, on your need, so fast for one meal. You don't want to be too comfortable.

When the ritual's done, eat what you want, straight away. When you're fasting, don't stop drinking water for obvious reasons. You should only skip a meal if you're healthy enough to do so, and check with your doctor first. If you can't skip a meal for medical reasons, or because you feel like you're going to pass out, try your best to eat a while before the ritual, so that you are approaching hunger, rather than feeling stuffed to the windpipe with cream cakes when it's time for your magick.

If you habitually shave any part of your body, it should be clean-shaven on the day you perform the ritual. This is about feeling clean and prepared, the way you would before an interview or a night out, rather than being a bit dishevelled. If you don't habitually shave anything, you can be as hairy as you like, because that won't feel dishevelled to you.

Who wants to prepare when you can do magick? Do this right, and the magick's going to work. Miss it out, and you'll wish you'd taken some extra time to get it right. Or take a risk, like other readers did, and see if you can get away without the preparation.

I think this preparation helps to make you experience the magick. It feels like an event, something that's happening for a reason.

In the other book, I described a protection ritual, and I know many people love to protect themselves before doing any magick, with banishing rituals. You can do that if you want to, but you don't *need* anything other than the ritual that's described. The protection comes from the Elemental Circle you create in your mind, and the pathworking you perform.

The Pathworking Method

You've made it to the chapter where I describe the ritual. If you use this magick, I hope you can see that everything that came earlier was there to make this part work. I don't get a kick out of typing, so those chapters all have a purpose.

If you've come straight here to try the magick, that's great – doing magick is more fun than reading about it. But if it doesn't work then read the earlier chapters. You might find a detail that helps the magick to work for you.

The Elemental Circle

This is where you perform magick. You've spent a few days building up to this, so you want it to feel like something is happening. In theory, you could do this while sitting in a public place, but it will feel better if it's something you do in a quiet, private place. A dark, calm and atmospheric room, at night, will get you in the right state of mind, but if you can't find that, anywhere will be ok.

An hour before you begin, dampen the noise; turn off phones, computers, the TV. Be alone, be quiet. Shut up and shut down. Make sure you've done the preparation described in the chapter called *Before the Magick*, unless you have a good reason to miss it out.

The pathworking relies on Elemental Imagery, and the opening of this ritual is a way of connecting to those Elements, warming up your imagination, and separating what you're doing from the ordinary day. Some people like to wear a big magick cloak and stand there with a massive staff of power, but I prefer to sit alone, dressed normally.

Everybody imagines differently, and if you find any of this difficult, I'll reassure you again that doing your best is enough. And do your best without strain. If you're sitting there with gritted teeth, forcing yourself to picture things, that's too intense. This should be easy.

To begin the ritual, create the Elemental Circle, picturing Earth, Air, Water, and Fire, encircling you. In some traditions, Earth belongs in the North, or The East or The West, and Air in the South or The East. You get the picture; there are lots of different ideas about where these Elements 'belong'. You may have a strong belief that you should face a certain direction and picture the Elements in very specific locations. For pathworking, you use a circle of Elemental Energy, so you can face any direction. You picture each Element in turn, and each Element encircles you, so the Elements are present all around you, instead of being in a single quarter.

In the pathworking itself the Elements are represented symbolically, in this order; Earth, Air, Water, Fire. That's the same order used to create the Elemental Circle. The method is straightforward.

With eyes open or closed, imagine a circle of Earth around you. How you imagine this is up to you. I usually see muddy soil and clay surrounding me in a circle about nine feet wide. It's not a disc, but a circle, like a line of Earth. It's as though somebody has taken handfuls of this clay and used it to draw a wide circle around me. (Some people prefer to use the word 'ring' instead of 'circle', as that makes it easier to picture. Use the word that makes sense to you.)

If you're standing in an apartment, on the top floor of a building, and if that apartment is small, it can feel difficult to picture this Earth as being in the room with you. It feels too out of place. This is why I usually imagine myself in an empty place. I picture myself standing on a desert plain, with a white sky, and that's easy for me. You can picture yourself anywhere you like, but it's usually easier than imagining the Elements being in your room. If you like to imagine the Elements in your room, and this really is what some people prefer, go for it. You can practice this before you ever perform a ritual and see what works.

If you can't imagine anything, you can think, 'There is a circle of Earth around me.'

You then picture this Earth transforming to Air. Picturing something invisible is difficult for everybody, so we usually cheat and picture something being *moved* by Air. I picture a circle of autumnal leaves being swirled around in a perfect circle by the Air. Other people picture a circle of mist, but I find that too watery. You can make up your own image for Air if it's meaningful to you. The circle of Air should replace the circle of Earth.

If you have a really bad imagination, you can think, 'A circle of Air surrounds me.' This one's quite abstract because we're surrounded by Air everywhere all the time, so how can there be another circle of Air? This is why I think it's useful to think of it as a moving, flowing breeze, separated from ordinary Air. Sometimes, I imagine that even though it's separate from me, I can feel its fresh chill.

You now imagine the Air turning to Water, and this is where I imagine the Air sublimates and splashes down to the ground, settling into a ring of Water. It's like somebody has dug a trench, a shallow, circular trench a few inches across, (with the circle itself about nine feet wide), that surrounds me, and the Water circulates there, clear and glittering. I like to picture the Air gouging out the trench as it turns to Water, but it doesn't have to be as dramatic as that. You can forget about Air and picture the Water in place around you. If you can't picture anything, think, 'There is a circle of Water around me.'

Water transforms into Fire, and for this I see the Water darken before igniting. It's like imagining the Water has turned to oil, before bursting into flames. Some people don't do that, and let the Water vanish and then be replaced by flames. I like to see the flames as quite low, a few inches high, so that I don't feel like I'm surrounded by an inferno, but some people picture a thick wall of flames. Practice and preference will help you decide what works for you. If you can't picture anything, you can think, 'A circle of Fire surrounds me.'

You might find this really easy, or difficult and confusing, but it's something that takes about twenty seconds. It shouldn't be any more difficult than picturing a few images or thinking the words that mean the same thing. You can worry about getting it right, or do it and see how powerful it is. You might be surprised at how quickly it feels like you've opened the way for magick. The circle is not a protection in itself, (that is, it's not a protective shield like many magick circles are), but it means that the method of pathworking that follows will let Elemental Imagery bring you the right demon, safely.

The Pathworking Ritual

Contact with the demon is achieved by reading each line of the pathworking beneath the demon's sigil, thinking of the demon's name, and then breathing onto the demon's sigil using the Elemental Breath described earlier. This is not difficult.

Imagine you are playing with your niece, and she asks you to be a dragon. You can imagine breathing pretend fire onto her toy castle to burn it down. If you're not the playful kind, imagine instead what you do when you breathe on a very cold window. You breathe onto the glass, knowing that condensation will mist over the glass. The Elemental Breath can be like this; you know that the image is being transferred from you into the sigil with your breath.

You picture the image, and if it takes several breaths in and out to get the image clear that's ok, and then when you are ready, you think the demon's name for a moment (as though 'speaking' it in your mind), and then let the pathworking image leave you as you breathe out onto the sigil. The image passes from you to the demon through this Elemental Breath.

Do not focus on trying to get the image out of your mind. It's ok if there's still some there; you are not trying to empty your head. It's like throwing half a glass of water on somebody. They get wet, and you still have water in your glass. If the image is still within you, trust that it has also been passed to the demon.

To reiterate, you breathe out onto the sigil, knowing that the pathworking image is *within* your breath, and is communicated to the demon *through* the sigil. If you can, keep your eyes open as you breathe onto the sigil. If you aren't able to do that, look at the sigil for a moment before making each Elemental Breath.

You know that by breathing a pathworking image into the sigil, you have taken one step closer to the demon and that the demon has been drawn closer to you.

For the first demon, Bael, you would read the line, *The remains of burned branches on a slab of white marble.* You keep breathing normally as you let yourself imagine this image. It might take a moment or up to half a minute. You get whatever image you can. If you can't see anything other than the words, that's ok too, as you've generated the image within yourself through reading the words, even if you don't have the imagination to see the image itself. You now think the demon's name, Bael, as though speaking it in your mind, and then breathe onto the sigil, knowing that the image of *burned branches on a slab of marble* is being passed through your Elemental Breath into the sigil. The demon is aware of you.

You would then read, *The sound of laboured breathing*. This is not an image, as such, but think of it as an image because it is formed in the imagination. You might actually hear laboured breathing, or you might think about laboured breathing. When you feel ready, think the name Bael once more, and breathe your imagined sound of laboured breathing into the sigil.

You do the same for the next two images, and when you have thought the name Bael for the fourth time, and breathed the image of *a white sky that becomes orange with sunrise* into the sigil, Bael will be present.

Some people feel or sense nothing until this final breath. Others feel a pull to the demon with each breath. You might feel nothing at all. You might find it difficult to breathe images out, in which case practice this technique. It's not hard so long as you're not hard on yourself.

You now make your request with a final Elemental Breath. You came up with a phrase earlier, so run through that until you can feel it. Again, think the name Bael, and then 'speak' the request in your mind, and then breathe that request into the sigil. You will be heard. Remain more aware of the demon than of your request itself. That means you shouldn't get lost in your own musings about your desire, but keep the demon in mind as you breathe your request out, knowing the demon is present. It usually takes one breath, but if you want to take a few more, that is ok.

That is pathworking. If this sounds weird - the idea of breathing out a request - it's easy if you try it. Imagine feeling really angry, and somebody tells you to take a deep breath and let it all out. It's like that. If you want, practice this with other thoughts and ideas before you try a ritual. Imagine something you want, and imagine breathing the desire out, onto any object, or into the air. Once more, if you aren't hard on yourself, and know that this is easy, it won't be hard.

It only gets difficult if you worry about whether you're doing it wrong. Knowing that is the most important practical aspect of this magick.

It's best if you breathe onto the sigil with your eyes open, but if you can't, look at it for a moment before making the Elemental Breath.

Your request has now been made, so you close the ritual by releasing the demon. You do this by looking at the sigil and 'speaking' the demon's name three times in your mind, knowing that this gives the demon the power to leave. Close the book, and it's over. You don't need to do anything to get rid of the demon. People love to spread scary stories about demons lingering, and tell you to banish and call on archangels to help, but you don't need to do anything. Banishing won't mess things up if you're into banishing, but I don't bother with it.

There's no summary because people read summaries instead of instructions. If you need a summary, you haven't learned the magick well enough. If it takes you more than an hour to learn something as easy as this, I'd be surprised. It could take five minutes. Once learned, it can be used with hundreds of demon powers to create thousands of results.

Pathworking The 72 Demons

There are seventy-two demons here, and they have many powers. In this book, I have listed only the powers that I know to work, as confirmed by many others. You will find other powers listed by different authors, and you can try them, but don't blame me if they don't work.

Sometimes, you might get an inspired feeling that a demon has a power that isn't listed. You can try making a request to the demon and see what happens. Working with these demons is not dangerous, so I think if you're ever wondering whether to try something you should make your discoveries by seeing what happens.

On each page, you get the demon's name, but most demons have many other names. This is because texts have been rewritten and corrupted over hundreds of years, so I used what I know to work or pathworking. If you want to see the other names, there's a chapter at the end listing all the alternatives. If you ever find you can't connect with a demon, try using a name that feels right to you.

I don't give any pronunciation guide for the names in this book, because the names come from an intermingling of languages, and they are often representations of how somebody thought the name should be written. That means there is no historically correct way to say (or think) the names. If you read the name and come up with a sound, it will work. As you work with the demon, you might find a different sound for the name occurs to you, and if so, pronounce the name that way in your mind. You never say the name out loud, but you still 'hear' it in your mind. This is a detail that's never worth wasting your time on. The sigil is like a demon portal, meaning any name that's remotely accurate will work. The only thing I'd say here is that the O sound in a name usually sounds more like AWE than OH, but you can be pretty easy-going about it all. You can look at the written name of the demon without even hearing it, and it will work.

The powers are described in short phrases, with a longer description then explaining how you could apply the power. What you get in this book is based on a grimoire used by a group of occultists that I belong to. I have expanded on those notes, tidied up a few points where relevant, and tried to make the powers clear without descriptions that are so long they become confusing.

If you look at the source documents, the listed powers barely resemble the powers you find in modern grimoires. The old books talk about 'good familiars' and powers to 'teach all Liberall sciences' and that sort of thing. The listed powers in this book are the powers discovered during hundreds of years of work, and a few decades of refined testing by practicing occultists. We've not modernised what was once written, but found out for ourselves the powers possessed by these demons.

For each demon, there is one sigil, enclosed in a circle. The circle isn't important except for helping you focus on the sigil itself. The sigils were redrawn by me, based primarily on the sigils in Sloane MS 3825 with some influence from Harley MS 6483, and some manuscripts shared with me and other occultists during the nineties.

Beneath each sigil, you get The Pathworking, written as four lines of descriptive text, used as described earlier.

When you get to the demon Bime, there are three sigils instead of one. This is because the sources often show two sigils and it's not clear which you should use. In some occult groups, this means people argue about which is the real sigil, or which is best. Bime is an amazing demon, so to make this easier for you I've given three sigils; sigil one, sigil two, and then sigil three contains both one and two. Which is best? I use the combined sigil, but some people don't. Have a look at them and use what feels right. Any of them will work.

There are about two hundred and fifty powers, so there are hundreds of ways to tweak, change, and transform your life, on the inside and on the outside, by affecting other people and by meddling with reality. If you've used magick before, you know this is possible. If not, I hope you're open-minded enough to try and to keep trying until you get the knack. It's easy.

And although I tenderly mocked people who do magick every day, I don't think magick is just about quick revenge, sex, money, and all the shallow pleasure you expect to come with a book of demons. This book contains more than that. Look at how the demons can be summoned to help you delve into the truth of who you are, and how you can connect with your unique powers and potential.

1. Bael

Compel silence. When somebody knows more than you want them to know, asking for their silence can often lead to them talking. If you have secrets that need to be kept, direct this power at the one you want to silence. They will keep your secrets as well as you do.

Proceed with stealth. If you wish to be somewhere without being seen, use this power. It can be used when you wish to listen in on conversations, enter places you are not meant to be, or mingle in a crowd where you are not welcome. An extremely useful power for those wise enough to know when it should be used. Direct the ritual at a specific event, project, or time period.

For apathy. If somebody is obsessed with you, your work, or another project that you want them to lose interest in, this power will make them apathetic.

The secret veil. If you have a secret that you wish to hide from one person or a particular group of people, this power will create illusions and disturbing thoughts when anybody tries to perceive the secret. Even accidental discoveries of your secret may be dismissed or forgotten as they will create unpleasant feelings in those who perceive your secret.

Cause anxiety. If you have an enemy that is confident and calm, undermine their power by creating anxiety. They will not know the source of their anxiety, but it will disable their ability to live well. Useful for revenge or to limit the effectiveness of an enemy during a competitive time. The effects of the ritual are temporary, lasting only a few weeks, but in that time sufficient damage can be done that the person develops an anxious personality. Only use this on somebody when there is no plan for reconciliation.

The Sigil of Bael

The remains of burned branches on a slab of white marble.
The sound of laboured breathing.
The smell of freshly dug soil.
A white sky becomes orange with sunrise.

2. Agares

Learn with ease. There are many powers that assist with learning, but this is especially useful when you want to learn a completely new skill, such as a language or instrument. When you are starting from the beginning, or at an early stage in your study, call on this power to ensure your learning is made easy.

Work with purpose. When you call on this power, it will enable you to see the value and meaning in your work. This can help you avoid burnout and disillusionment. If your work lacks meaning and is detrimental to your life, you will see that clearly, so be aware of the risk.

Ruin reputation. This will make an enemy act in ways that make them appear like an idiotic and indulgent fool to all who know them. The effects may be brief but should cause a lasting loss of reputation.

Make somebody return. This power is said to 'bring back runaways', but it is useful to influence anybody you wish to come back into your life, whether a lover or a family member.

Stimulate decision and action. When somebody else needs to make a decision and act on it, for your plans to succeed, use this power to make that person make a decision and act in the way you want them to act. This is most effective when the decision is almost made, but the person is hesitating through fear.

Weaken magick. This will not only weaken the magick of somebody but will make others see them as weak. Used against a random occultist, it will have no effect. There should be an emotional connection. Either you know them, or they have caused you harm. In such cases, it works.

The Sigil of Agares

A black leafless tree in front of a red sunrise.
The sound of lustful moaning, as from a drowsy orgy.
The scent of a rose.
Distant, reddish lightning in a dark evening sky.

3. Vassago

Find a lost object. The power to find a lost object is granted by other demons, but when working with Vassago, the power is best used on an object that has been lost for a long time.

Discover truth. When you suspect that you are being lied to, this power will lead you to discover information that reveals the truth.

Know the past. If you are tormented by an incident in your past, either because you are bitter about somebody else's actions or guilty about your own, use this power and then think about the situation during the following weeks. Through intuition and glimpses of information, you will sense the greater truth and understand why something happened. It sounds like therapy, and that's how people use it. It's a way of releasing stored pain, confusion, or uncertainty about the past.

Sense change. When you suspect change is coming to a relationship, at work, or in any area of your life, this power will help you get a feeling for what the change may be and how you could prepare.

The Sigil of Vassago

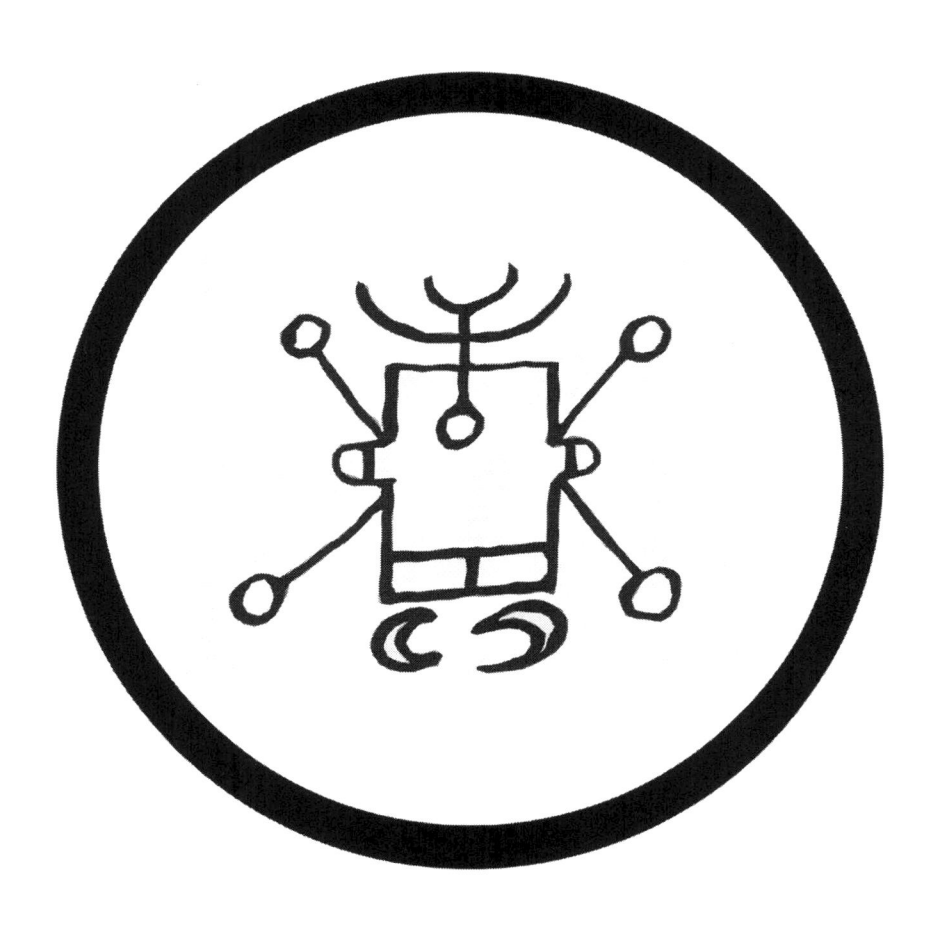

A frozen pond, its surface scattered with red leaves.
The sound of many feet on gravel.
The taste of blood.
A yellow sky warms to amber as a white sun rises.

4. Gamigin

Overcome grief. The power of Gamigin is often described as an ability to know the dead. This is not communication with the dead, but understanding and release. If your grief lasts too long, use this power to gain a full appreciation of the person you loved, and this will help you overcome your grief. There is no harm in grieving, but when it goes on too long, this power can bring relief.

Write convincingly. The power will improve your writing generally, but is highly effective when you aim to improve the persuasive qualities of your writing, without sounding as though you are trying to persuade. If you believe what you are saying it produces better results than when being deceptive.

The Sigil of Gamigin

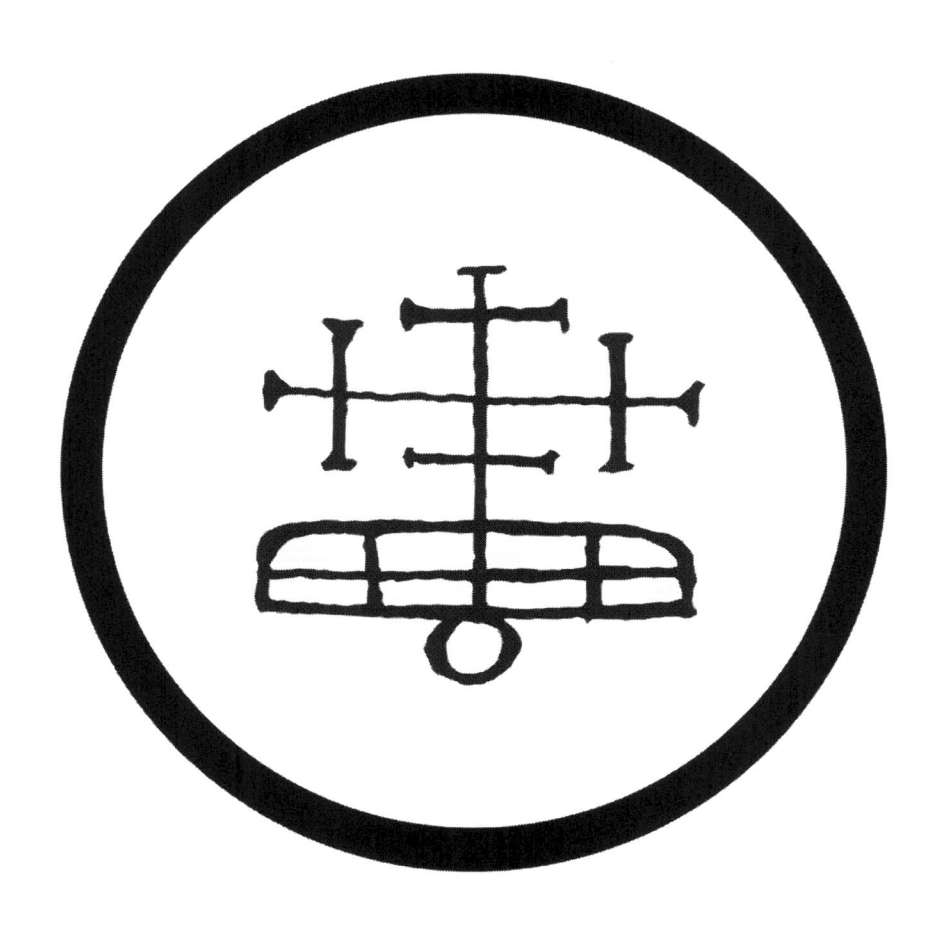

An old woman in rags holding a dead crow.
The sound of a waterfall.
The taste of smoke.
A pale blue sky with a golden sun.

5. Marbas

Cast a glamour. In magick, a glamour is a veil of illusion that makes you appear to be something you aren't. Use your imagination to choose whatever would be most useful, but this is often used to appear braver, more attractive, or more competent, and used strategically. A glamour is usually cast on yourself, not on somebody else, but you may obtain some success when using this to make somebody else appear in a way you want them to appear. This could be done in secret, to help a friend, or to make an enemy appear in a manner of your choosing.

Cure infection. It's questionable whether you need magick to cure infection when modern medicine is usually effective, but if you find you have a persistent or recurring infection, use this power to seek a rapid cure.

Cast infection. Cause somebody you dislike to become unwell, with an infection that will be difficult to cure.

Discover answers. If something is happening behind closed doors, use this power to find answers regarding the situation. This isn't divination, but a way of knowing what other people are doing without telling you, and seeing how it will affect you. Although you might get an instant answer or feeling during the ritual, you should think about the situation for a few minutes each day for a week or two, or until you're satisfied with the answers. Do this without the expectation of answers arising, and answers will arise. Sometimes, it may be minutes or hours later, but you will perceive more truth than was otherwise available to you.

The Sigil of Marbas

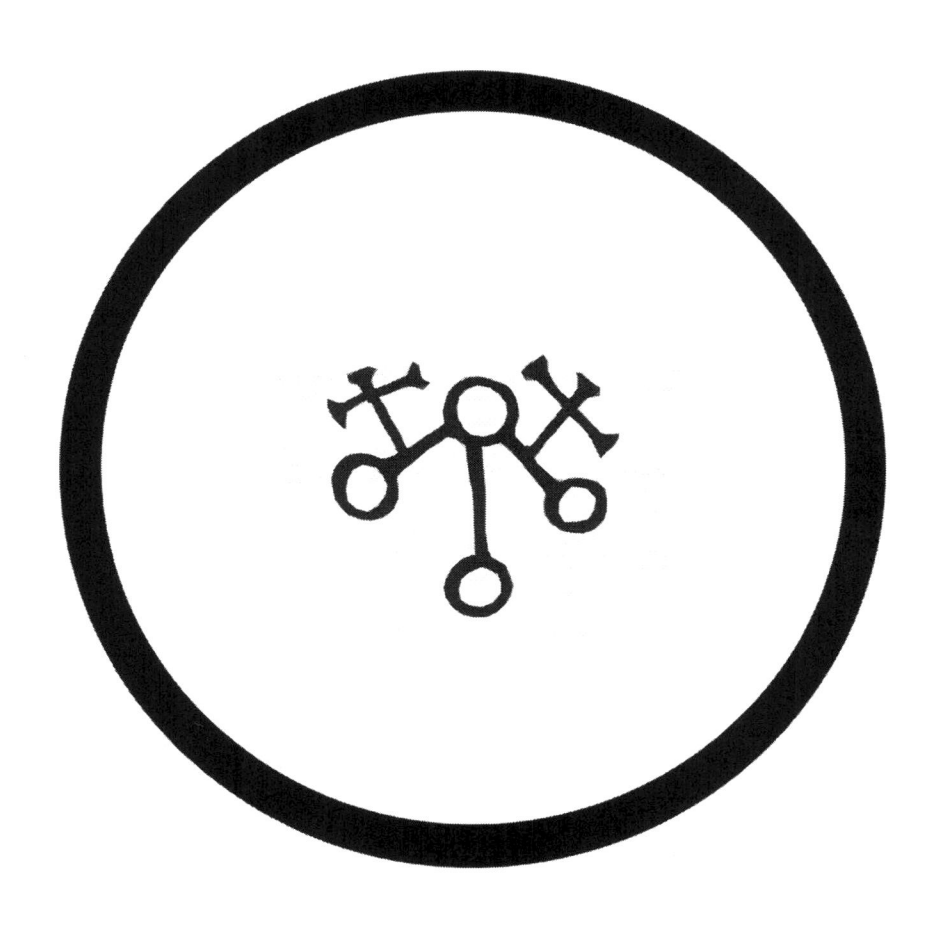

A tree of white blossom on a green hillside.
The sound of many feet on stone.
The scent of animal fur.
In the deep blue sky, a full yellow moon.

6. Valefar

Stimulate disloyalty. This power preys on a person's weakness and will make them give in to any temptation they have to betray their partner, their employer, or anybody they choose. If they are completely loyal (which is rare) the result will be discomfort and not disloyalty.

Perceptive wisdom. When you have already studied a situation for a long time and remain confused or unable to progress, seek perceptive wisdom, so you can see all that you need to know and understand the situation with wise perspective. You will be required to put in the time to think about your problem in the hours and days following the ritual, but as you do, clarity will come quickly.

Break secrecy. If you suspect that somebody is withholding a harmful secret from you, this power causes them to confess or let the truth slip out.

The Sigil of Valefar

The silhouette of a young woman before white sunlight.
The angry barking of many dogs.
The smell of rain on grass.
A white sky fades to yellow.

7. Amon

Stimulate romantic feelings. Cause somebody you know as a friend to feel romantically toward you. This is a power of influence and can cause feelings that are not true to the person's actual desire. This means that the attraction will be temporary unless something genuine arises.

Break friendship. Cause two friends to become enemies in a short period of time. You can also use this against lovers and business partners, but the strongest effect is on friendship. It cannot be used to break your own friendship.

Reconcile friendship. Unlike the above power, this can be used to reconcile your own friendships. It can also be used to make other people reconcile. It can be used to reconcile lovers but is less effective than when used on friendship.

Inspire awe. This power is used to make an enemy see you as awe-inspiring. Your aim may be to frighten or to convert the enemy into a friend, and your intention should be clear when you perform the ritual.

Create chaos in a group. In any small group of people, where friendships hold the group together, you can bring a chaotic blend of fear, mistrust, and jealousy. This can work on groups who work together in business, but only if friendship is a core part of their relationship. It can be used as a punishment against enemies by destroying their friendship group.

The Sigil of Amon

A white dog, its fur wet with blood.
The sound of wind rushing through bare trees.
The smell of burnt hair.
A white sky becomes blue as the white sun rises.

8. Barbatos

Understand what a person means to you. When you meet somebody, or know somebody and want to deepen the relationship, you can use the power as a form of divination. You will find that you gain a much deeper understanding of the person and whether they are worth your time. Knowledge and emotions may come quickly or over a few weeks.

See the truth behind secret actions. When you suspect somebody is keeping secrets, you can use this power to see what is really going on. Secrets are concealed in many ways, from occult powers to basic lies. This power doesn't bring truth, confession or help you discover a way to access withheld information, but improves your intuition, so you know what somebody is keeping secret. It works best when you suspect a person of being secretive, but can also be used generally, to gain an understanding of all that's been withheld from you, by everybody you know. If you're sensitive, it can be overwhelming. If you're not sensitive, you might only gain a few ideas and impressions about what's being hidden.

Gain intuition about what's about to happen. If you feel like change is coming, or if you know change is coming and you aren't sure what to do, this will help you guess, intuit, or sense what's coming your way, to help you prepare.

Be respected by those in power. Anybody who believes they are above you will be made to respect you and your work.

Understand science. If you're studying science, this power has immediate and obvious value.

The Sigil of Barbatos

A black leafless tree in blue moonlight.
The sound of laboured breathing.
The smell of freshly dug soil.
A white sky becomes red.

9. Paimon

Understand inner needs. Knowing what you really need at this time in your life is one of the finest powers. The knowledge lets you work on what will benefit you the most. After the ritual, a strong awareness of what you really need may occur to you, sometimes immediately, but often over several days. Remain open and think about your life during this time to allow the magick to work.

Develop reputation. When you work with money, in areas such as banking and investment, Paimon can help you develop a good reputation. This power can also be used when you want others to invest in you and your projects. The power has been used successfully by many start-ups and artists.

Influence through presence. This power makes you more able to influence another person to take on your ideas, trust you, or follow you as a leader, when you spend time talking to that person. The effect will last until that person experiences great personal change.

Confuse somebody. Create a sense of confusion in one person that you know. The effect lasts for several days, so timing this is important if you want an advantage.

Musical ability. Paimon will bring creative inspiration to musical performance and composition. You can ask for this power to sustain you during the upcoming years.

Remove weakness. To obtain control of your personality, you can remove a weakness. If you believe you have a personality trait such as laziness, you can ask Paimon to remove that trait. Your habits may remain in place after the ritual, even when the trait itself has been removed, so avoid acting habitually and allow the change in your personality to settle into you.

The Sigil of Paimon

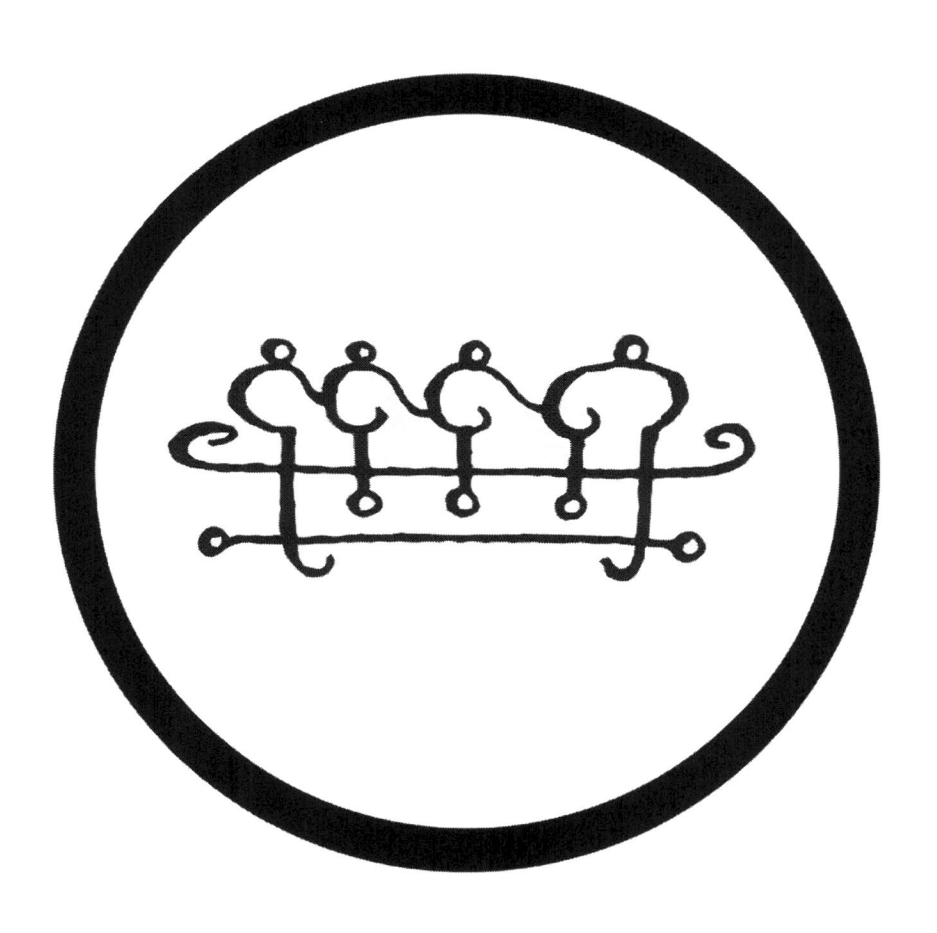

The silhouette of an old man before a white morning sun.
The sound of metal being hammered.
The smell of burning wood.
A white sky with a faint crescent moon.

10. Buer

Mental and emotional healing. At any time when you feel that you need to be healed, because of mental stress or emotional distress, Buer can bring a sense of calm certainty that makes you feel protected and safe. In this state, your healing can progress.

Understand law. When you need to understand a legal situation, call Buer to assist. This is not a power used by lawyers, but by ordinary people who need to understand how to cope when a legal situation arises. This can work on anything from a problem with your mortgage, to being sued, or when facing court for any reason. If you need a deeper understanding of the situation, Buer will assist.

Clarify intense desires. If you suspect that a strong desire is becoming obsessive, you may wish to see the true nature of your desire. This applies to obsessive pastimes, as well as relationships that may be infatuation-based. Use this ritual, and you will see whether your obsession is something that will assist you or something that will drain and distract.

Subdue anger. Use this power to calm your anger, if you are going through a stressful time that makes it difficult to control your anger. You can also subdue anger in another person. Extremely angry people may sense that they are being subdued and will become angrier in retaliation. That makes this power sound risky, and it is. If the person you wish to subdue is only annoyingly angry or has occasional outbursts, the ritual will work. If the person is habitually angry, the ritual might bring more rage, so use something else to curse, bind, or remove that person from your life.

The Sigil of Buer

A white goat's skull with black horns.
The sound of many hissing snakes.
A smell like wet straw.
A white sky becomes grey as a scarlet sun rises.

11. Gusoin

Bring respect. Use this to make a person, or a group of people, respect you and all that you say. You can also use this to make enemies respect each other. This is especially useful if you have friends who are divorced but stuck in the angry phase. If you use the magick to make them respect each other, it makes life easier for everybody.

Sense emotional potential. When you meet somebody that you like, or when a relationship has begun, this power can help you sense the future of your feelings for the person who currently attracts you. This can save you time if you don't feel much, or it can help you nurture the relationship if you sense that it's valuable.

Loosen the tongue. This power will make somebody who is secretive become casual with their secrecy, so that you can obtain strategic information. This is most useful when used against a work colleague who knows more than you, but it also affects personal relationships.

The Sigil of Gusoin

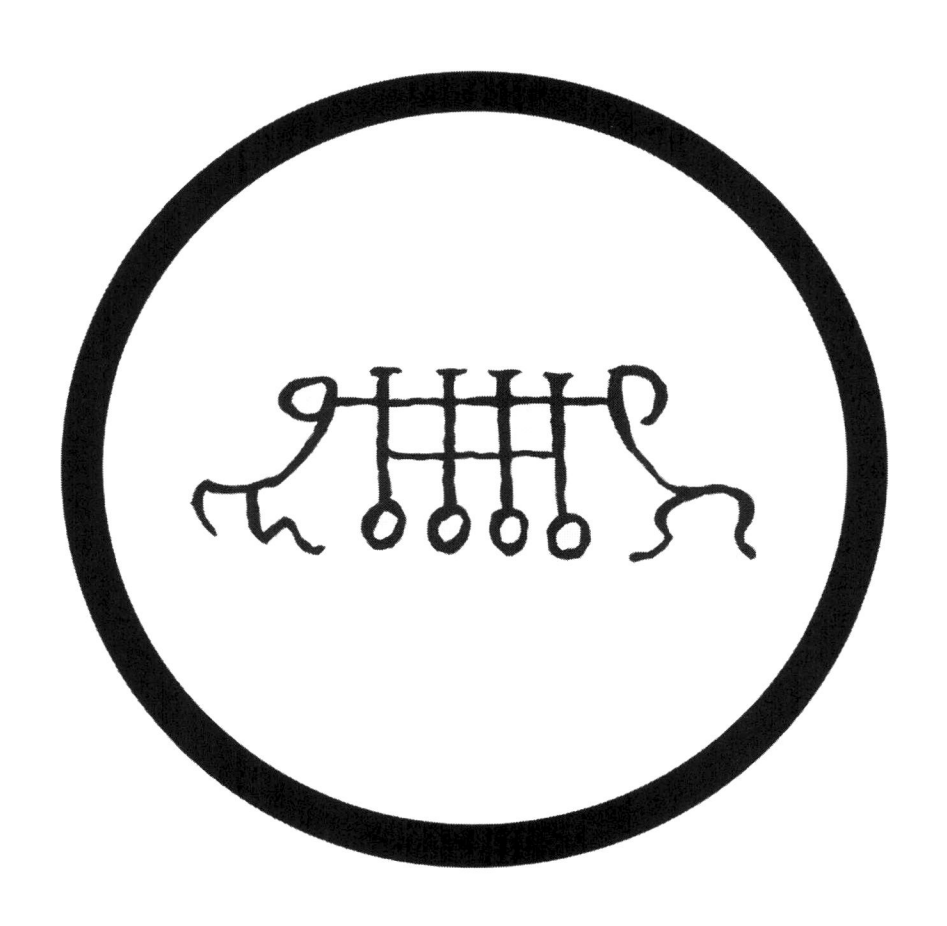

Ivy covers a flat stone in an empty field.
The sound of many people breathing in sleep.
The odour of mould.
A black sky becomes white with clouds.

12. Sitri

Urge somebody to leave. Make somebody leave your home, or make a neighbour leave your street or building. This can take time and will work on that person's weakness, so be patient and let the power find a creative way to bring about the outcome.

To incite temptation. When somebody is attracted to you, this power can bring up feelings of temptation that will distract that person like an itch, until it is scratched. Don't assume that because you've used magick, you have the right to seduce somebody, but use this to make attraction advance into something more lustful.

For sexual passion. This can be used in a relationship to make it more sexual and experimental, or it can be used with somebody you have only just met. It won't work if there's no attraction, but if there is it will speed up the potential for passion. Passion is often more than sex and can conjure intense feelings in both people (because you are intertwined with this magick as well).

To appear sexually desirable. Everybody wants to be desirable, but this power is about appearing as though you are somebody who is filled with confident lust, without appearing desperate or needy. That appearance can be potent and will have an effect if there is any potential for attraction. You can ask the spirit for this appearance of desirability to be general and ongoing, or for a particular occasion, or to be seen this way by a particular person. Sitri is the most popular demon for seduction and can bring astonishing results, but will not work if you sit at home, or if you wait to be approached. Sometimes, Sitri will make others approach you in a social situation, but don't rely on such occurrences. With the power in place put yourself in situations where you can use your confidence and magnetism.

The Sigil of Sitri

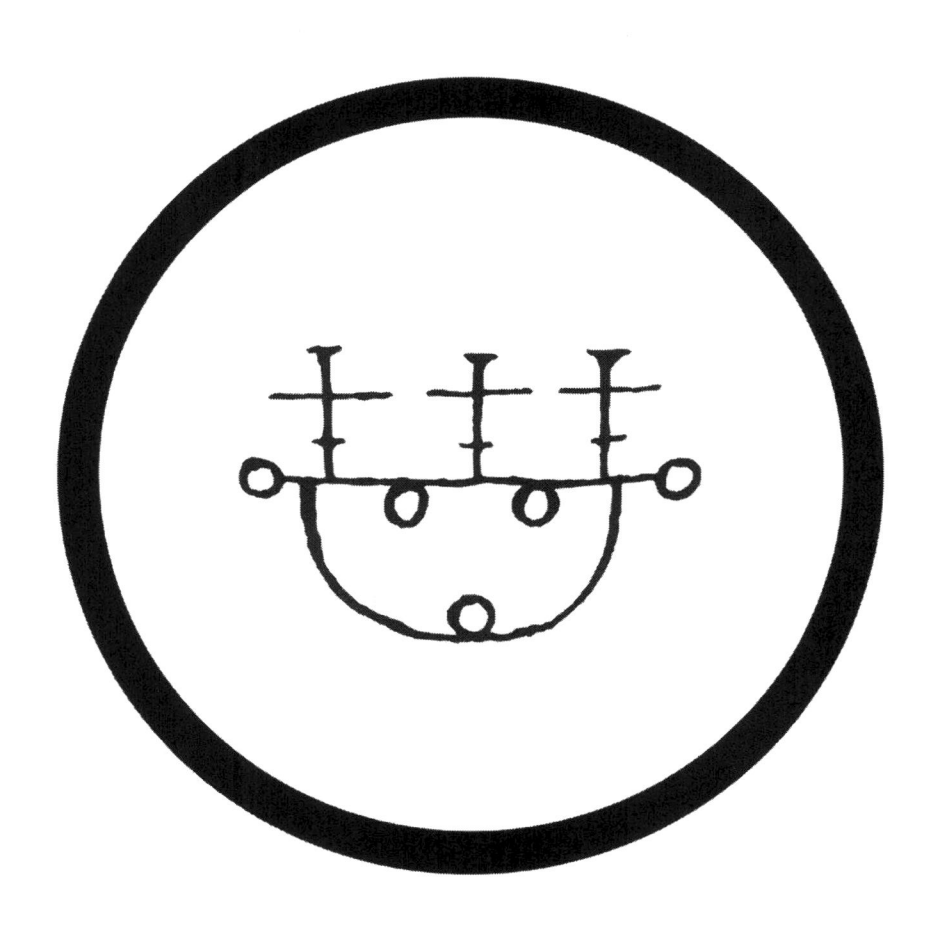

A pregnant old woman holding a wooden staff.
The sound of lustful moaning, as from a drowsy orgy.
The scent of a rose.
A white sky becomes rosy with pink sunrise.

13. Beleth

Encourage lust. When you are in a relationship, this power encourages your partner to be lustful more frequently. It also encourages a more experimental lust, enabling you and your partner to explore new depths of sexual pleasure.

Love from lust. When you are in a passionately sexual relationship but wish for a more emotional partnership, use this power to allow the emotions to be as present as the sexual feelings, both in yourself and your partner. If love is possible, you will have more chance of seeing that truth when your emotions are as present and intense as your desire.

Sex magick. If you use sex magick of any kind, call Beleth to improve the intensity of all your sex magick. If you don't know of any sex magick, the simplest method is one of the best. Hold your desire in mind while you have sex, and allow your desire to be obliterated by orgasm. Forget about the desire, and you get the result. If you want to try that, use the power of this ritual to empower your sex magick before you attempt the sex magick. You can do this a week before, or immediately before. You are asking Beleth to make your sex magick more intense and successful, and when you actually perform sex magick, you do not need to think about Beleth at all.

The Sigil of Beleth

A pond frozen like clear glass with filthy water beneath.
Birdsong.
The smell of hot iron.
A sapphire sky softens to yellow.

14. Leraye

Increase mental strength. When your intelligence is required for a demanding and ongoing project, you need mental strength. This gives you the capacity to be persistent and effective, without burnout.

Reveal enemies. There are several methods for finding enemies, but this one works when you suspect there is an enemy, but you are having difficulty finding out who it might be. The demon will cause other people to gossip and spread rumours which should reach your ears. You can then choose how to act when you discover your enemy.

Cause conflict. Use this to cause an individual to face conflict from all the people who would normally be trusting. The power can also be used to create conflict within an organisation or group of any kind, breeding mistrust and urging people to express their darkest suspicions.

The Sigil of Leraye

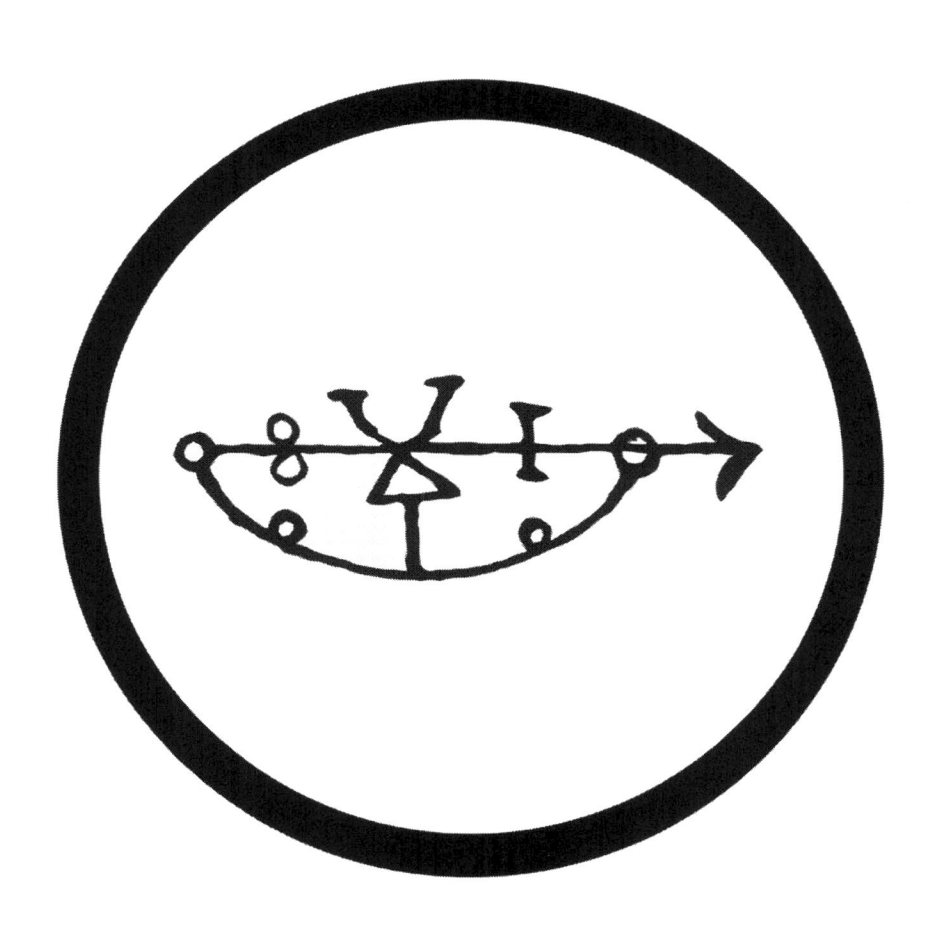

Under moonlight a river runs red with blood.
The sound of a cloak falling to the ground.
The odour of mould.
A white sky becomes blue as a yellow sun rises.

15. Eligos

Know enemy plans. With all this talk of enemies, you might think this sounds like a book about military strategy. To ignore the strength of enemies is to make yourself vulnerable. If you feel you have no enemies, wait until you are successful. As you grow in stature and reputation, enemies arise to bring you down. If you know their plans, you can defeat them. When you know that enemies are working against you, call for Eligos to make their plans clear, so that you can work in a way that outwits or avoids trouble.

Blind affection. This power is used to win the affection, admiration, passion, or love of somebody who is socially or financially superior to you. It's been said that this is a power to help you sleep with your boss, but I think that's to underestimate how helpful this can be when you need the attention or affection of somebody who would normally be out of reach. You will need to interact with the person, so only use the magick if you are in contact with somebody of a higher status.

The Sigil of Eligos

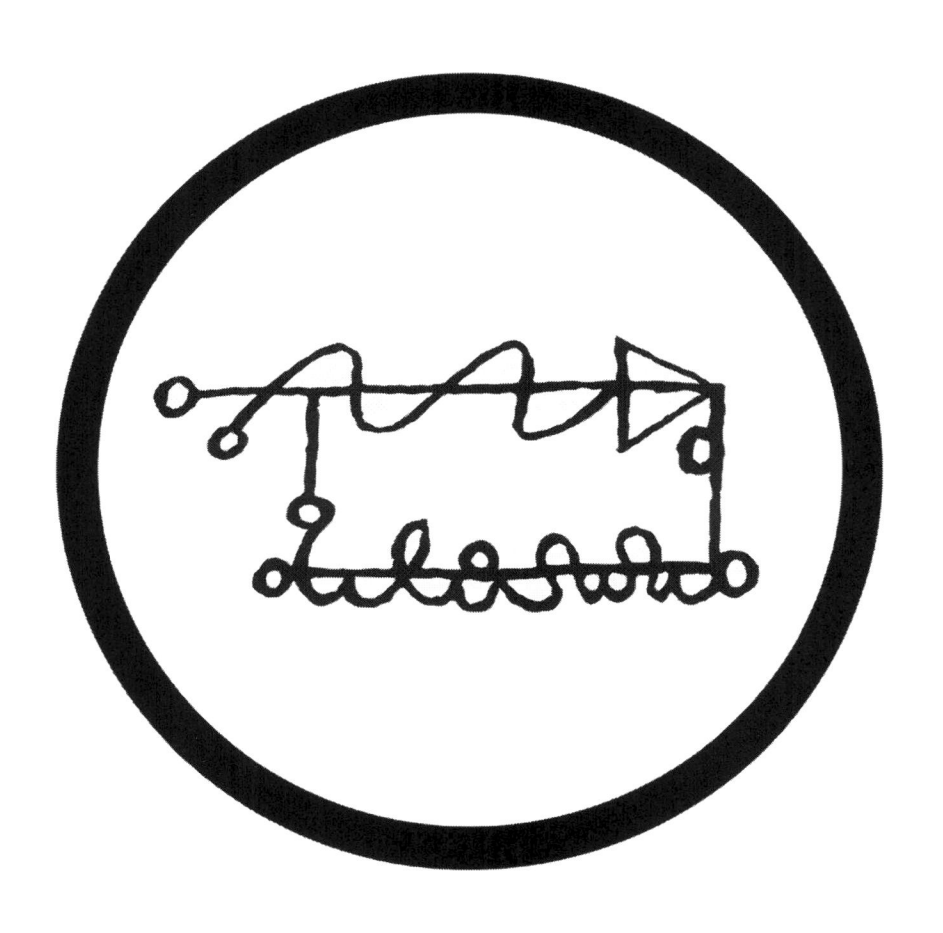

Rain turns the dry hillside into a river of mud.
A low humming close to your head.
The taste of honey.
From a russet darkness grows a deep amber light.

16. Zepar

Make somebody infertile. This needs no explanation except that it will not cause permanent infertility, but it will make conception far less likely for those you target.

Romantic passion. The powers of Zepar are often described as sexual, and ideal for seeking a one-night fling, but I believe this is misleading. Zepar can make you more likely to attract love, and can also be called to influence somebody you know to become passionately romantic.

The Sigil of Zepar

A leafless tree filled with silent crows.
The sound of many feet on stone.
The scent of a distant storm.
A grey sky warms to deep red as a yellow sun rises.

17. Botis

Cause disfigurement. The power does not cause literal disfigurement in most cases, although it can cause rashes and similar outbreaks. It is more likely to create a glamour of disfigurement, so that somebody looks far less attractive than usual. There are countless ways this can be used, from punishment to weakening another at a strategic moment.

Read thoughts and feelings. Use this power to know the mind and heart of a person you already know quite well. After the ritual, contemplate the person without expectation and you will gain insights into their thoughts and feelings. When you next meet, you may find that you are able to read the truth behind the words and actions of the person.

Courage. When you need courage for a specific situation, which may last hours or weeks, this power can give you that courage. When you use this power, you will also find you are more persistent when pursuing a goal, and this is widely believed to be a consequence of the courage you feel.

The Sigil of Botis

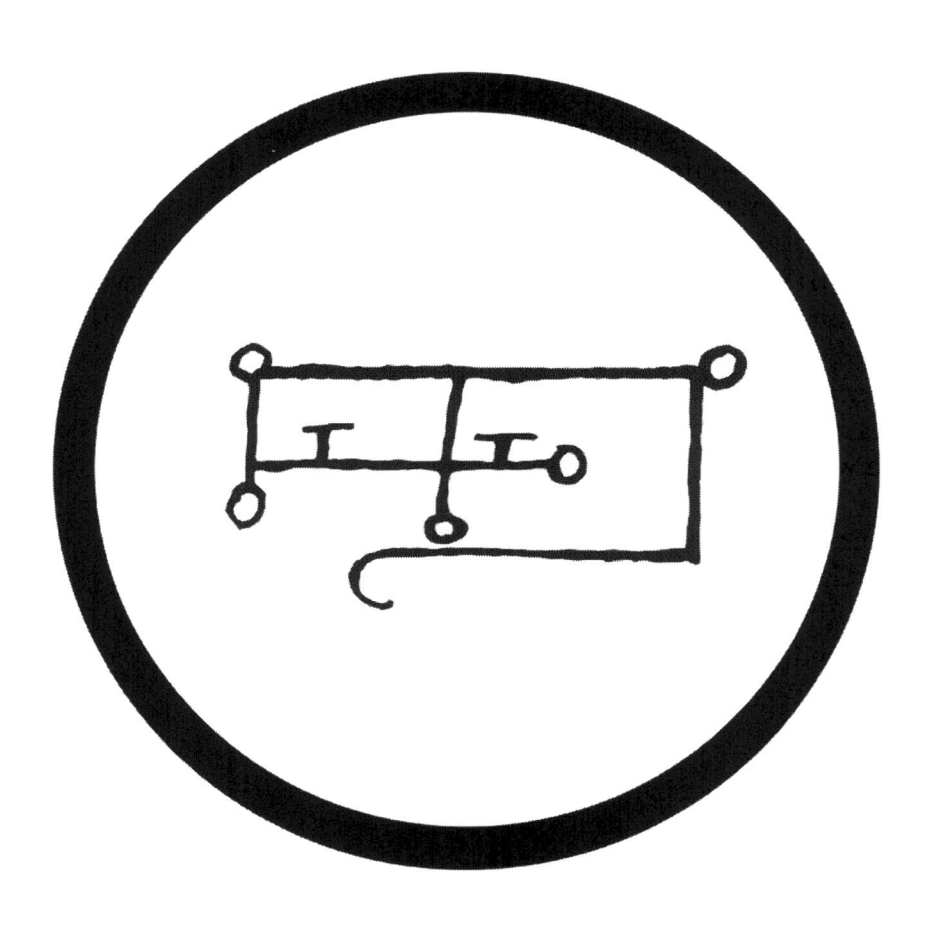

An eagle overhead in a stormy sky.
The sound of metal being hammered.
The smell of a stagnant pond.
White lightning in a stormy evening sky.

18. Bathin

Safe travel. This power can make a journey safe and free of delays. Although used by most people when they are making a long journey over several weeks, it can be used for a single day of travel, if that journey is important or potentially perilous.

Financial calm. When you are about to make a financial decision, such as buying a house, making an investment, or any other major and long-term plan, use this ritual to give you calm perspective. This power takes the emotions away from you, enabling you to see the true potential of your decision, rather than your immediate excitement and hope. It doesn't sound like fun, but it's better to make a good financial decision than one driven by giddy urgency.

The Sigil of Bathin

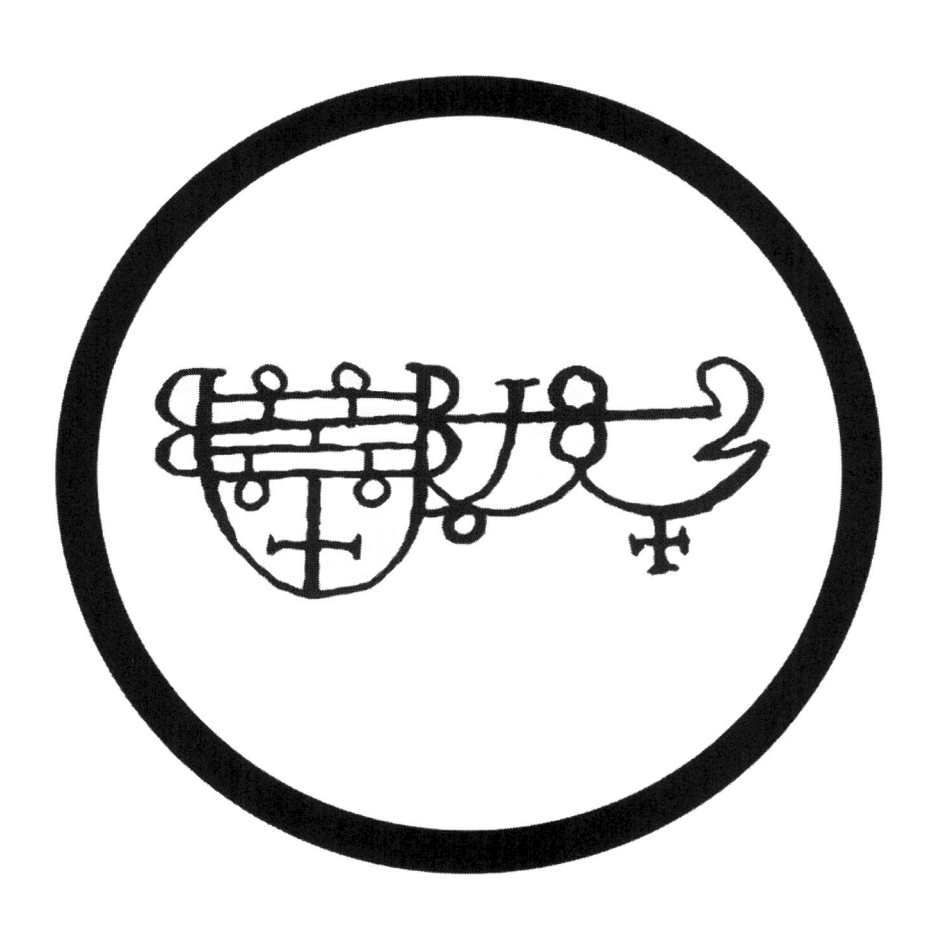

Seeds sprouting green from black soil.
Birdsong.
The smell of burning wood.
A cobalt sky dims to black.

19. Sallos

Create a captivating aura. If you wish to be appealing to strangers that you meet, use this power to give yourself a captivating aura. It makes people want to be near you and makes them feel that you are special. When you are this captivating, the intrigue that people feel will often make them attracted to you.

Passion from affection. When you are in a friendship that feels more like attraction or passion to you, use this power to make the other person's affection transform into passionate love.

The Sigil of Sallos

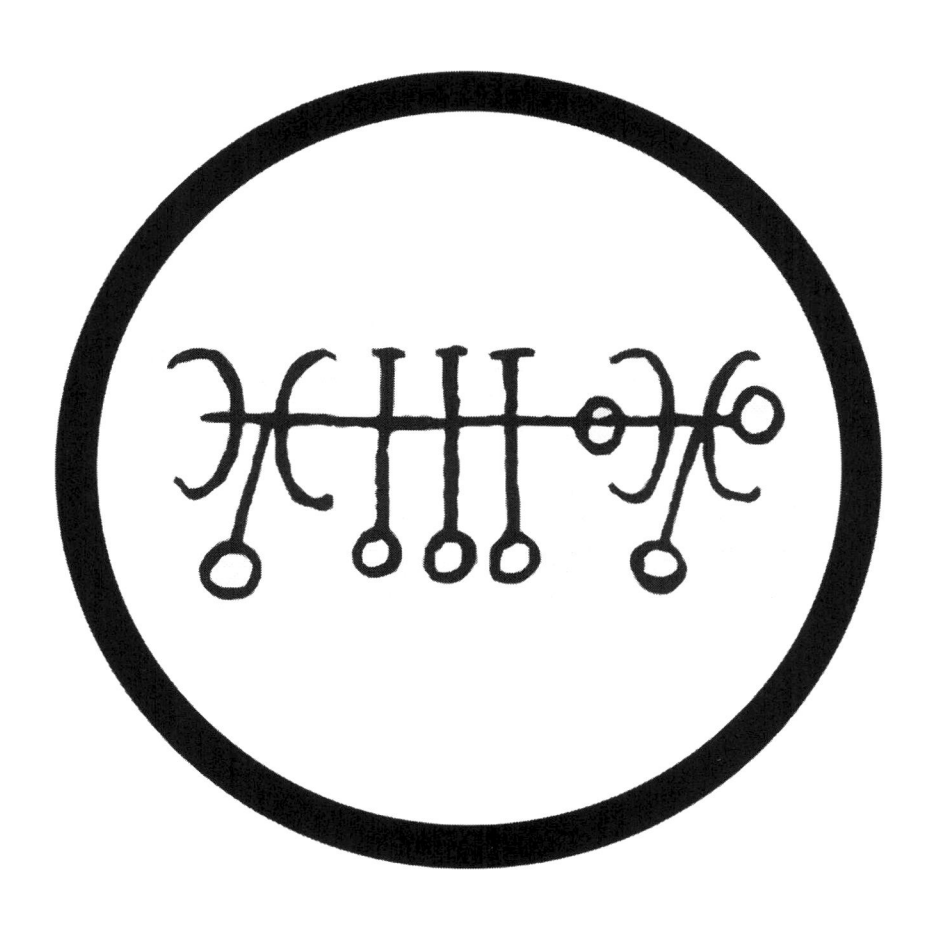

The bones of a horse in dry, yellow grass.
The sound of a waterfall.
The smell of rain on grass.
A dim red sun behind misty cloud.

20. Purson

Explore change. If you are stuck in some way, you need change. This is true for personal situations as well as more general problems in life. When you feel like a situation has become unchangeable, use this power to see how best to bring about change. The insights you gain in the days following the ritual may be extremely simple or may involve complicated plans and magickal strategies. Remain open-minded and assume that a pathway to change will become clear.

Attract investment. When you need investors for a project, this power will make your ideas appealing to people with money. You will still need to do the work of putting your project in view of investors, and when you do, you will receive more favourable responses.

The Sigil of Purson

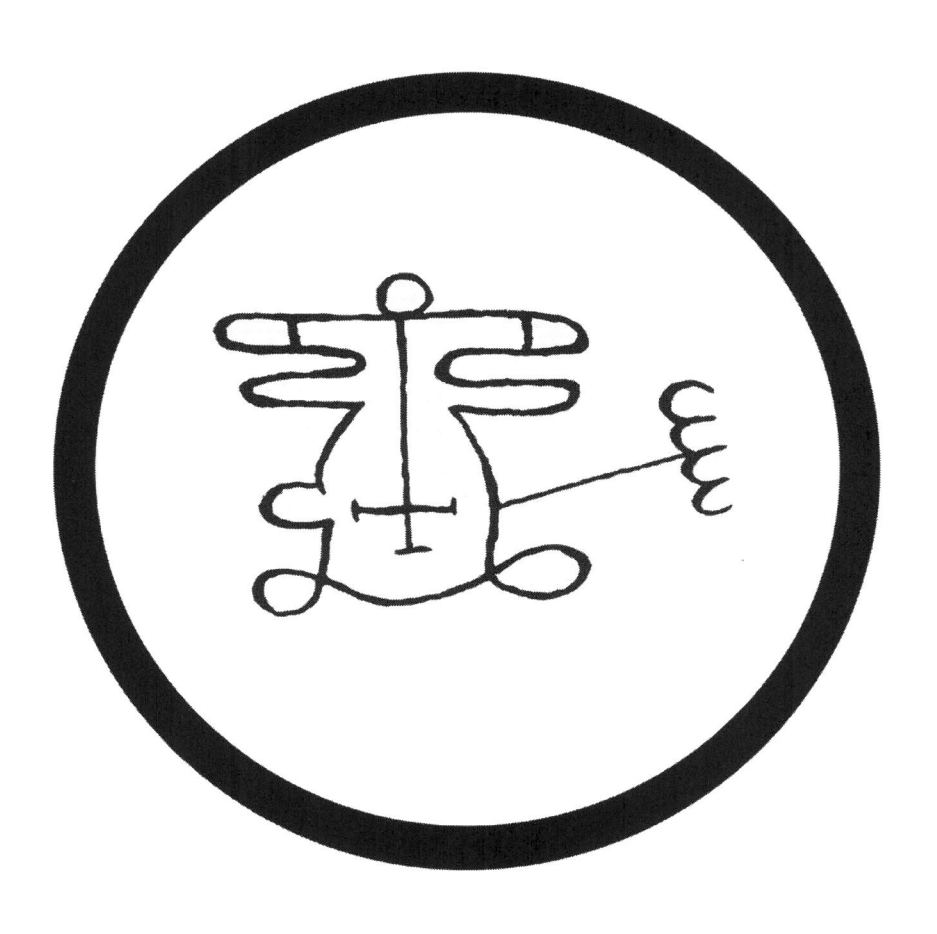

At night, the edge of the forest alight with flames.
The sound of laboured breathing.
The taste of blood.
A dim, white full moon showing through cloud.

21. Marax

End procrastination. Procrastination can be an annoyance or something that wrecks your life. Call on Marax to make you approach activities without fear or dread.

Gain an overview. Many problems seem too difficult to understand until you see the big picture, and get an overview of how the problem fits into your life. This power enables you to see if a problem is something that needs all your attention and concern, or is something that will pass without much effort, and without great impact on your life.

Financial credibility. Whatever area you work in, you often need to convince other people that what you do is financially credible. This power makes other people see your work as something that could help them make money if they invest in your talents or abilities.

The Sigil of Marax

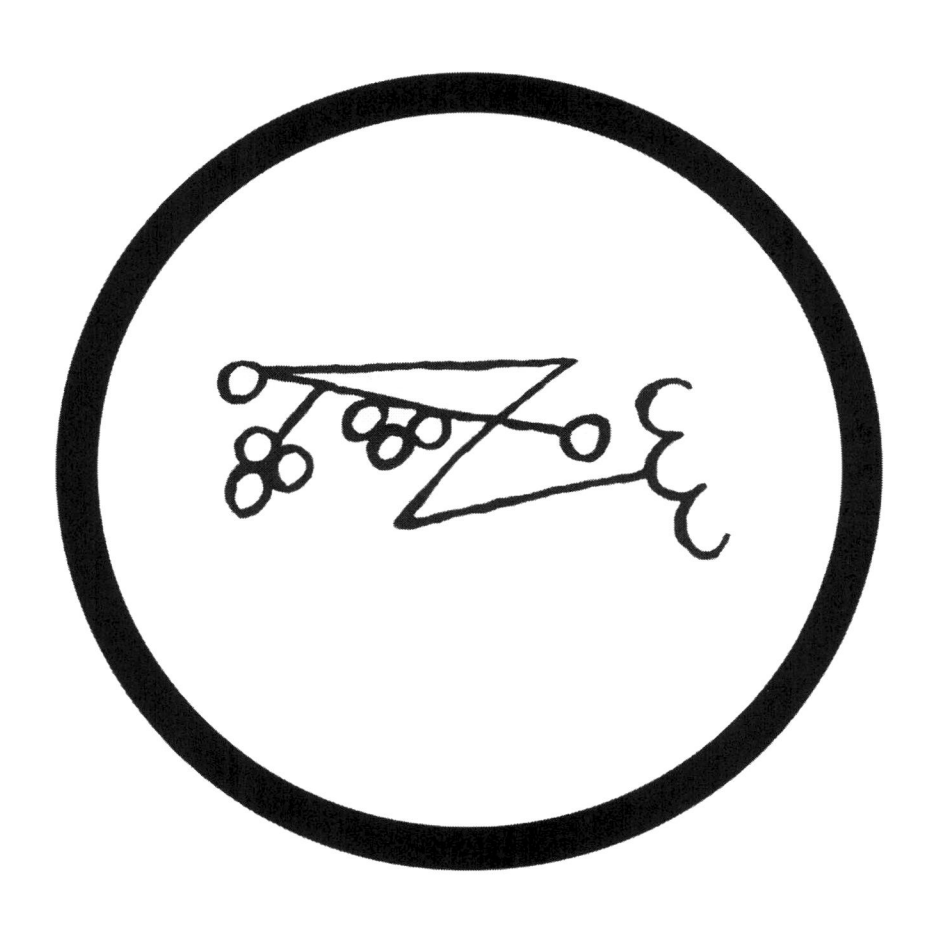

Sunlight through morning mist over a sodden field.
The sound of many people breathing in sleep.
The smell of burning wood.
White lightning in a pale yellow sky.

22. Ipos

Be convincing when you speak. This will make you appear charming, likeable, and able to convince others. You can use it for an important occasion, or to make yourself generally more convincing. It convinces without making others resist, or feel they've been persuaded, which makes you seem less threatening.

To be more charismatic. It takes practice and interaction with others to be charismatic, but if you are going to socialise, this power can make you have more charisma, which gives you more confidence without making you appear pushy or egotistical.

Remain brave when attacked. If others try to make you appear stupid, weak, or in any other way inferior, one of the first things you lose is your courage. Being attacked can make the strongest person feel weak. If an attack weakens you, or makes you a victim of your own anger in response, use this power to become brave, determined, and steadfast.

Make another have courage. You can use this when somebody else is holding you back through lack of courage. It may be a spouse or business partner, but if somebody lacks the courage to join you in a venture, this will give them the courage to join you. It isn't a form of influence or persuasion, but it will remove the barrier of cowardice. There may be other things you need to work on to get your way.

The Sigil of Ipos

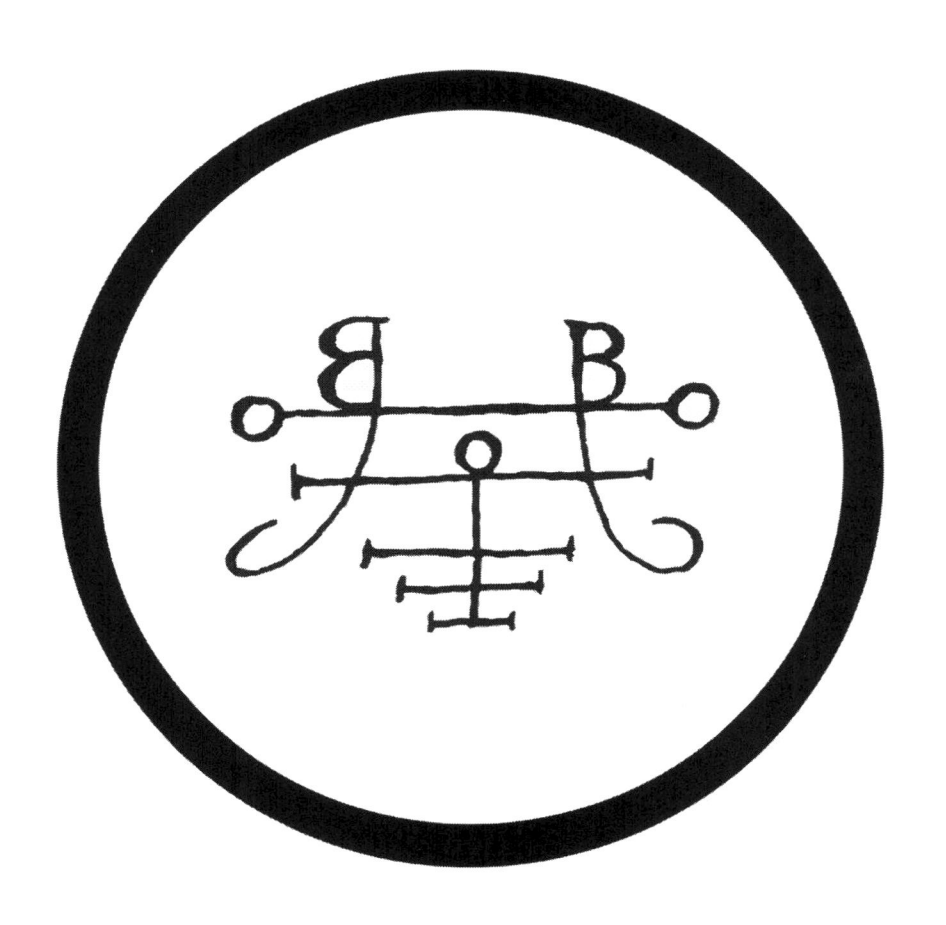

Fish bones in watery mud.
The sound of many feet on gravel.
The smell of crushed leaves.
A pale yellow sun behind a sheet of white cloud.

23. Aim

Intelligent courage. Courage can lead to rash actions and is best when controlled and guided by intelligence. When faced with a frightening or stressful situation seek the power of intelligent courage, to enable brave but wise decision-making.

Disrupt home life. Direct this power at one individual, rather than a household or couple. That individual will then find their home life is disrupted by arguments and angst. This magick may affect several people to bring the result, but works strongly when your intention is to bring the disruption to an individual.

Random accidents. Cause somebody to experience a series of minor accidents that wear a person down.

The Sigil of Aim

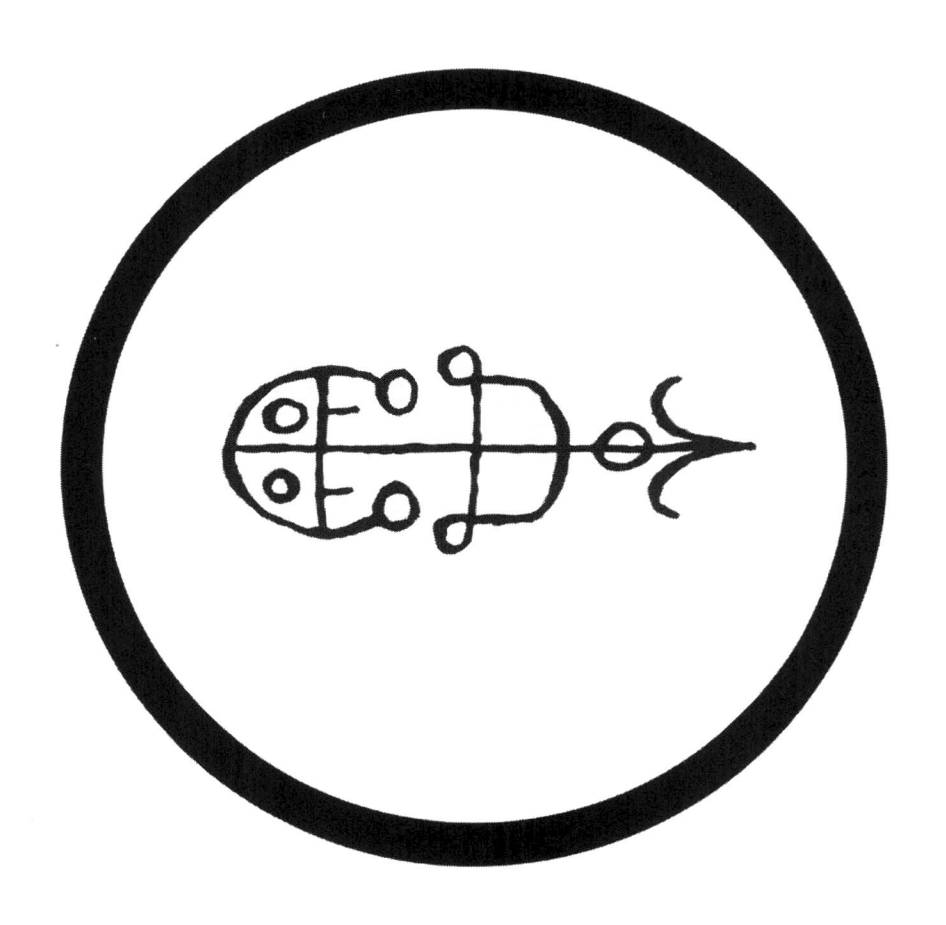

A jawbone at the edge of the ocean.
The sound of a cloak falling to the ground.
The taste of charcoal.
In a deep blue sky, a white crescent moon.

24. Naberius

Create confusion. Confusion can be caused by many demons, but with Naberius it is easy to define where and to what degree you wish confusion to occur. Cause anything from intense confusion in one person to mild confusion in a large group, for the length of time you define, or in relation to a particular event or subject.

Casual deceit. When you have lied or deceived another in any way, you may need the power to convince another of your innocence. This is more for casual secrets made in your personal life, or at work, than for major legal problems.

Discard a reputation. If you have developed a reputation that is not to your liking, whether deserved or not, cause others to forget the reputation you have and form new judgements based on what they experience when in your company.

The Sigil of Naberius

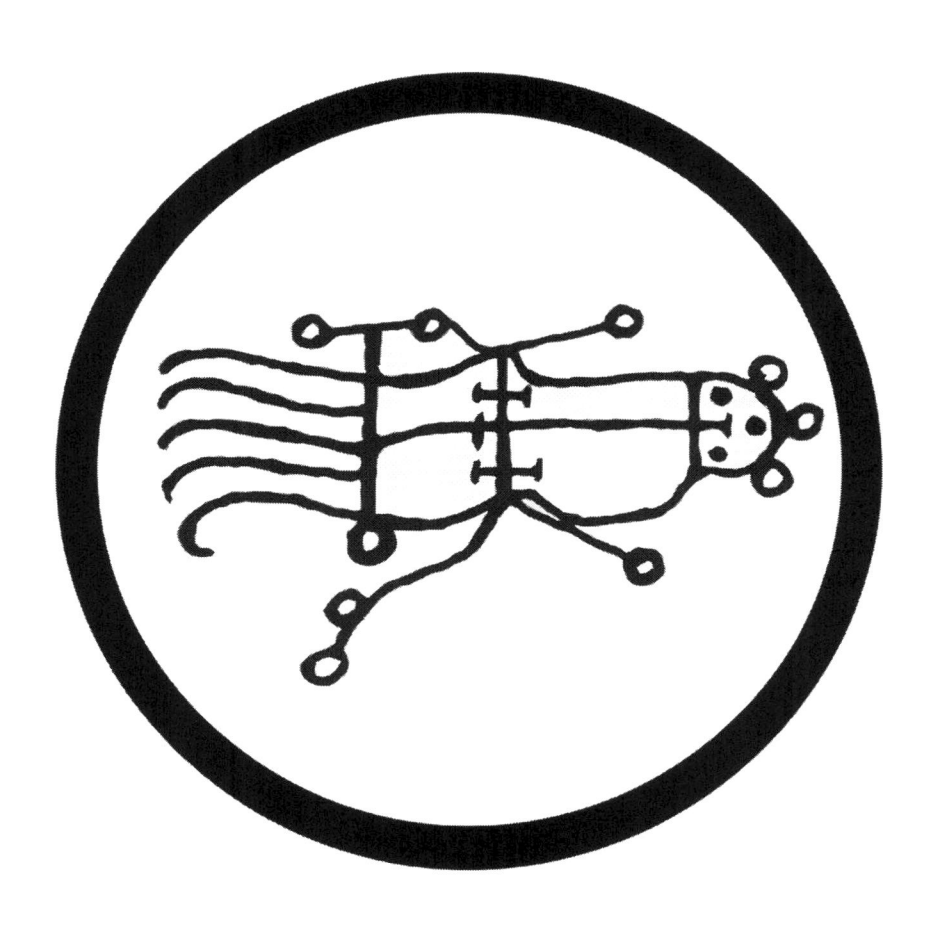

A circle of warm cinders in a dry, empty field.
The sound of many hissing snakes.
The smell of burnt hair.
A deep blue sky becomes black and filled with stars.

25. Glasya Labolas

Cause sickness. The power is used to make a person become unwell. You cannot control how the sickness manifests, but it is usually a brief and severe illness. In rare cases, it may manifest as a less serious illness that lasts longer.

Provoke attacks. Make a person more emotionally volatile and filled with violent anger. This can lead them to attack others, verbally and physically. How can this be of benefit to you? If you want to ruin that person's reputation, this is an excellent way. You can even get them into much more serious trouble. It is possible to ask the demon to provoke violence between two individuals, if you, for example, want to break up a friendship or partnership.

Cause loneliness. This power creates the feeling of loneliness even if the target remains surrounded by friends. It works by making the target feel rejected and unloved. A powerful curse, the only downside is that you may not see the result, because people have become experts at hiding loneliness in modern times.

Quantum leaps. If you work in any area of science or design, use this power when you feel your work has become uninspired or when your development is blocked. It will create a sudden leap of intuition that enables your work to progress.

The Sigil of Glasya Labolas

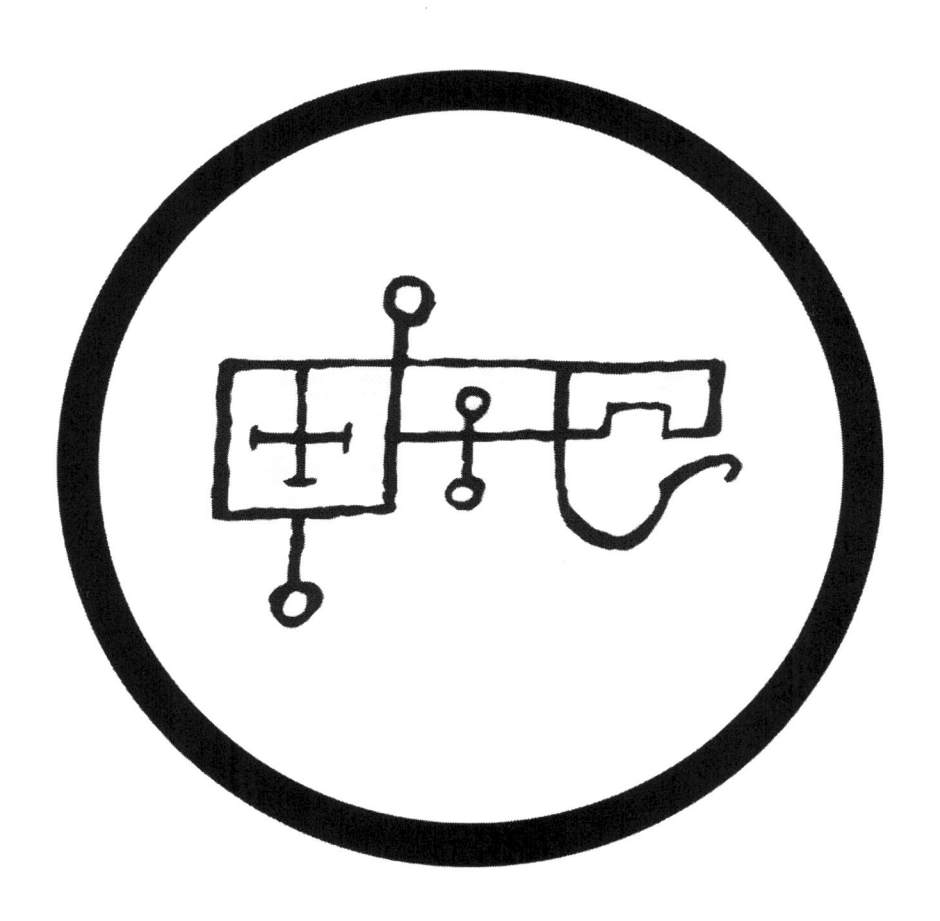

The black of a leafless tree before a starry sky.
The sound of metal being hammered.
The smell of crushed leaves.
White light darkens to a deep scarlet.

26. Bime

Business strategy. The most underestimated power of Bime is the power to help you develop a good business strategy. The demon can bring money, and people ask for money, which is fair and reasonable and detailed below. But if you're in business, or even better, starting a business, the wisdom, intuition, and strategic insights of Bime are far more valuable than any amount of money. The ritual does not need to be repeated endlessly but should be repeated whenever your strategy needs a major overhaul, review, or when your work changes direction.

Meet financial needs. When you feel a great need for money, Bime can provide much-needed money in a timely manner. And that means it may be fast, or it may come to you just in time. Look for opportunities but also remain detached and allow money to come from any place that it can come.

Obtain material wants. If there is something you want, use the ritual not to attract the actual finances required, but the desired outcome. If you want to buy a car, you need the financial resources to obtain that car, but your *desire* is the car. During the ritual, you would focus on the car, and ignore the money. Although you know the ritual is about finding sufficient money to meet your wants, it is by allowing the desired result *itself* to come about, giving no heed to money, that you are most likely to get what you want.

Flowing wealth. When you run a business or make money in a way that is not based on a wage, call for Bime to make wealth flow. This flow will increase over time. This is a ritual you may want to repeat once a year to empower such flow.

The demeanour of wealth. The rich can spot a poor person pretending to be wealthy a mile away. Buy the right clothes, wear the right watch, and you'll still be spotted because you haven't been around wealth. So what? Most of the time this doesn't matter, and flaunting wealth is rarely advisable. But if your progress depends on you appearing to be settled with your money, either to fit into a new social group or to negotiate with other wealthy people, use this power to appear at ease with your new wealth. It will give you the eloquence and sophistication expected by others. As you have probably guessed this power can be used when you become wealthy, but can also be used as a glamour, to appear wealthier than you are. There are many risks involved in using such a glamour, but if you require that power, it is available to you.

Understanding financial matters. When you start making money, you start hiring people to help you with money, such as accountants and financial advisors. Finding the good ones is difficult, and you need the ability to make good contacts and to know whether you are being guided and advised in a way that meets your needs. If this sounds like a minor power, it's one of the most important for wealth seekers. It's widely known that most people who come into sudden wealth, either through a win or an inheritance, lose every last penny. Money brings the responsibility to know how to live with money. Unless you develop an understanding of financial matters, the greatest gains will mean nothing. When your wealth increases, the wisest action is to begin planning for the future, rather than to live like the poor and spending everything you have from month to month. This psychological shift is difficult but vital if you are to sustain wealth, so use this power to give you the discipline, understanding, and resolve to make your money work for you.

Three sigils follow. Read the earlier chapter concerning Bime to determine which you want to use.

The First Sigil of Bime

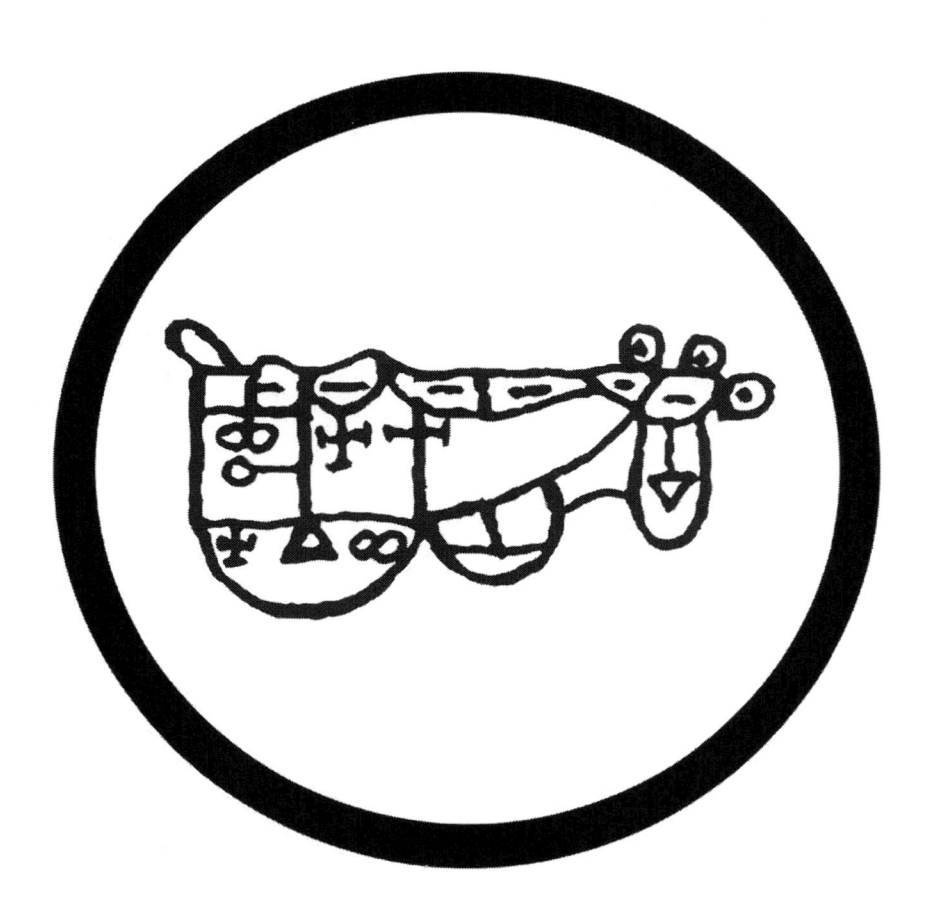

A glossy scorpion on orange sand.
The angry barking of many dogs.
The taste of charcoal.
An azure sky brightens to amber.

The Second Sigil of Bime

A glossy scorpion on orange sand.
The angry barking of many dogs.
The taste of charcoal.
An azure sky brightens to amber.

The Combined Sigil of Bime

A glossy scorpion on orange sand.
The angry barking of many dogs.
The taste of charcoal.
An azure sky brightens to amber.

27. Ronove

Appear safe. When you appear to be comfortable and safe, nobody will see you as a threat. You can then work against others without being suspected.

Appear trustworthy. Call on this power to make you appear trustworthy to any person that you deceive. The power works best when you are deceiving one person, rather than several.

Improved charisma. If you feel socially awkward, breaking that pattern is difficult without some degree of charisma and easy confidence. The demon can help you develop this style of charisma.

Directed charm. Direct this power at somebody you know and desire, and your efforts to be charming, through conversation and actions, will be seen as romantic, authentic, and alluring to them. Your objective level of charm and wit may not be improved, but the target of the magick will believe you are charming.

The Sigil of Ronove

A white tree laden with purple fruit.
The sound of laboured breathing.
Birdsong.
A white sky becomes pale blue.

28. Berith

Unwavering determination. When you have already made a decision to commit yourself to a project, this power will make your determination to succeed incredibly strong.

Conceal flaws. Even if you don't know what your flaws are, you can use this power to hide them from everybody you interact with. The effects are usually ongoing until you go through a period of change or personal development. The people who are close to you will usually see who you really are, so this magick is directed at all other people you interact with, in business, at work, and in general.

The Sigil of Berith

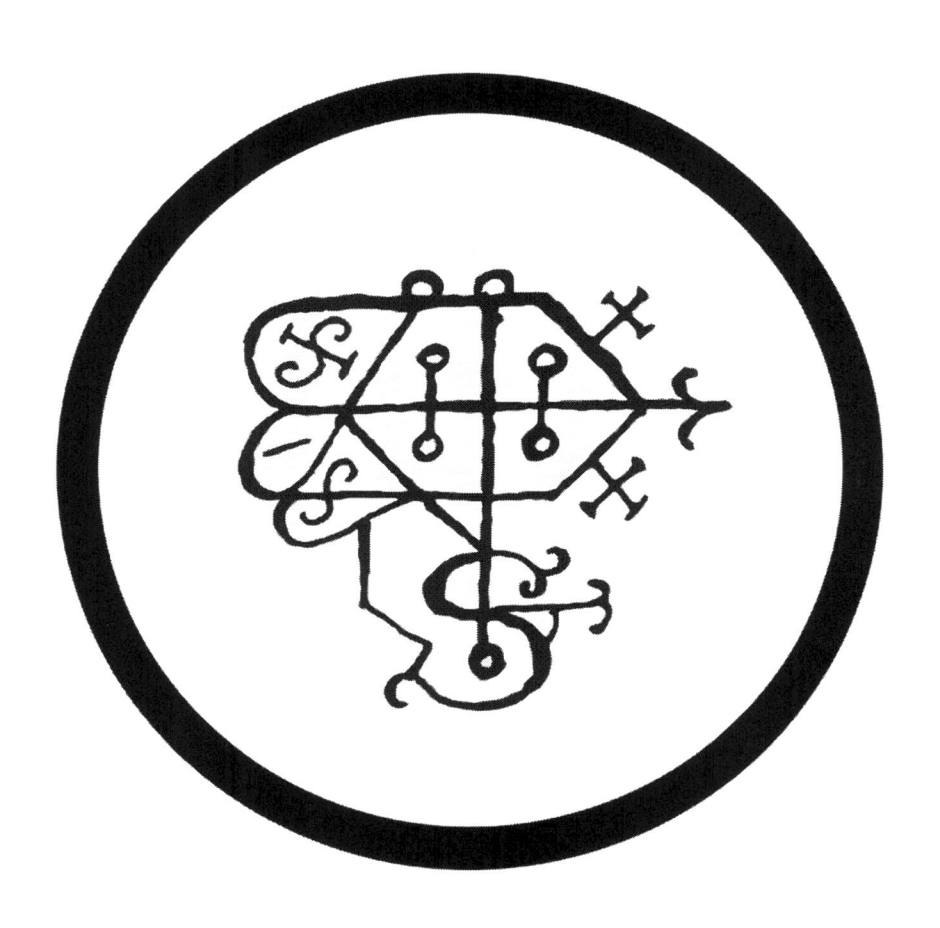

A fallen tree crawling with ants.
The sound of wind rushing through bare trees.
The taste of blood.
A pale blue sky with a crescent moon.

29. Astaroth

Practical insights. This is another power so often underestimated because it sounds boring compared to powers for money, illusion, or sex. The power to find practical solutions to any problem or challenge is one of the greatest powers in this book. Imagine being faced with a legal problem, or a decision that goes against you, or a problem in any area of life that seems insurmountable. You might charge all kinds of ritual magick at the problem, but unless you have examined the true nature of the problem and the practicalities, you may be wasting your time. This ritual will enable you to gain perspective on the problem so you can find the most practical solution. Sometimes that will be alarmingly simple, and sometimes it will involve detailed plans, and you may even get insights into which magick you should use.

Prolific creativity. If you work in any artform, and you want an exciting burst of creative inspiration, use this ritual to break into your unconscious desires for creative expression. Make sure you put aside time to work, whether you feel inspired or not, and that will make way for prolific and intense creativity.

Meaningful work. If your work feels like it is serving nothing other than your bank balance, and you seek more meaning and purpose, this power can guide you to find a more meaningful existence. It will not provide you with that existence but will let you see what it is that could give your life more meaning, and then it is up to you and your use of magick, to create a life where you can do that work.

The Sigil of Astaroth

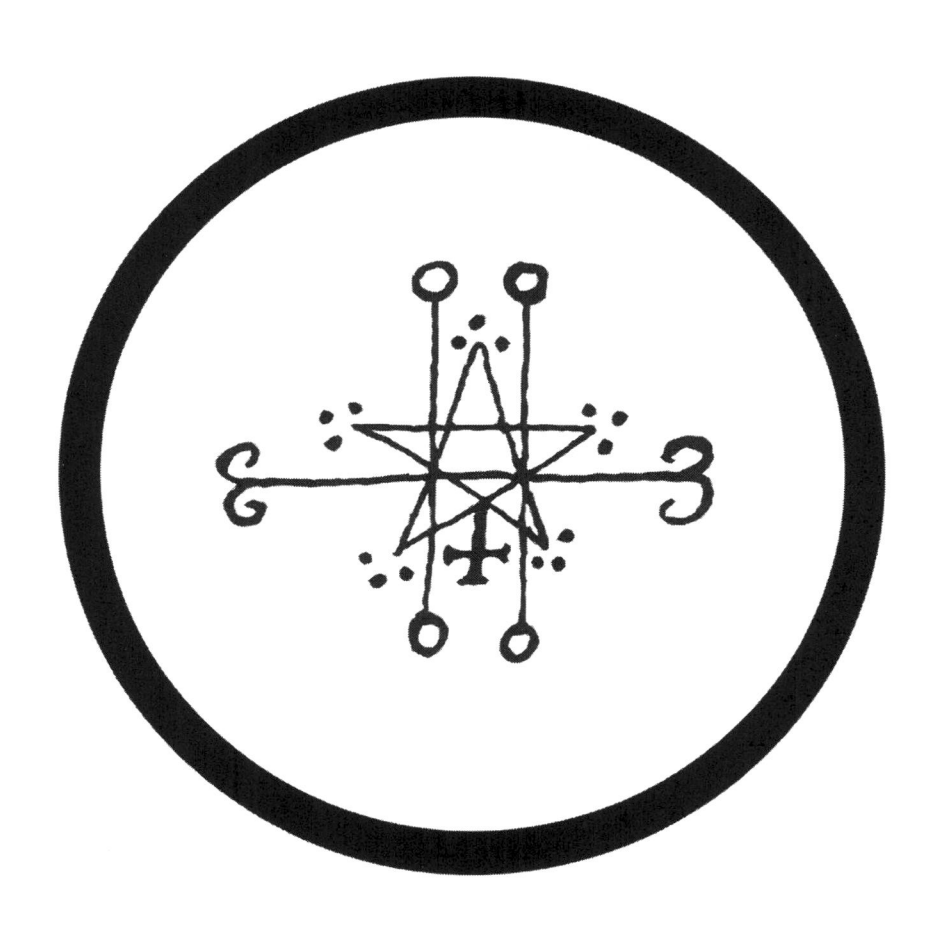

A black crack in a stone wall.
A low humming close to your head.
A smell like wet straw.
A pale pink sky with a golden sun.

30. Forneus

Make somebody fear you. This can be used on a stranger you've never met if you know their name. It is most effective when used on somebody you know well. The power will cause the arrogant or troublesome to become afraid of you. Be certain that fear is the sensation you wish to induce, because although it has many uses, fear can make people ineffective, defensive, and even violent, so use your judgment.

Creative reputation and fame. If you work in any creative area (it can be business, not just the arts), you can use the power to be recognised for your creative talent. Fame can be a result if you work consistently.

To appear powerful. This will make all who know or encounter you believe you are a person of great power.

To confuse all enemies. You can ask the spirit to confuse all your enemies, so they are filled with admiration for you. You do not even need to know who your enemies are. When enemies feel this admiration, they are weakened and confused. If you have a known enemy, then you can use this to put them off guard, and then use other rituals to defeat them as desired.

The Sigil of Forneus

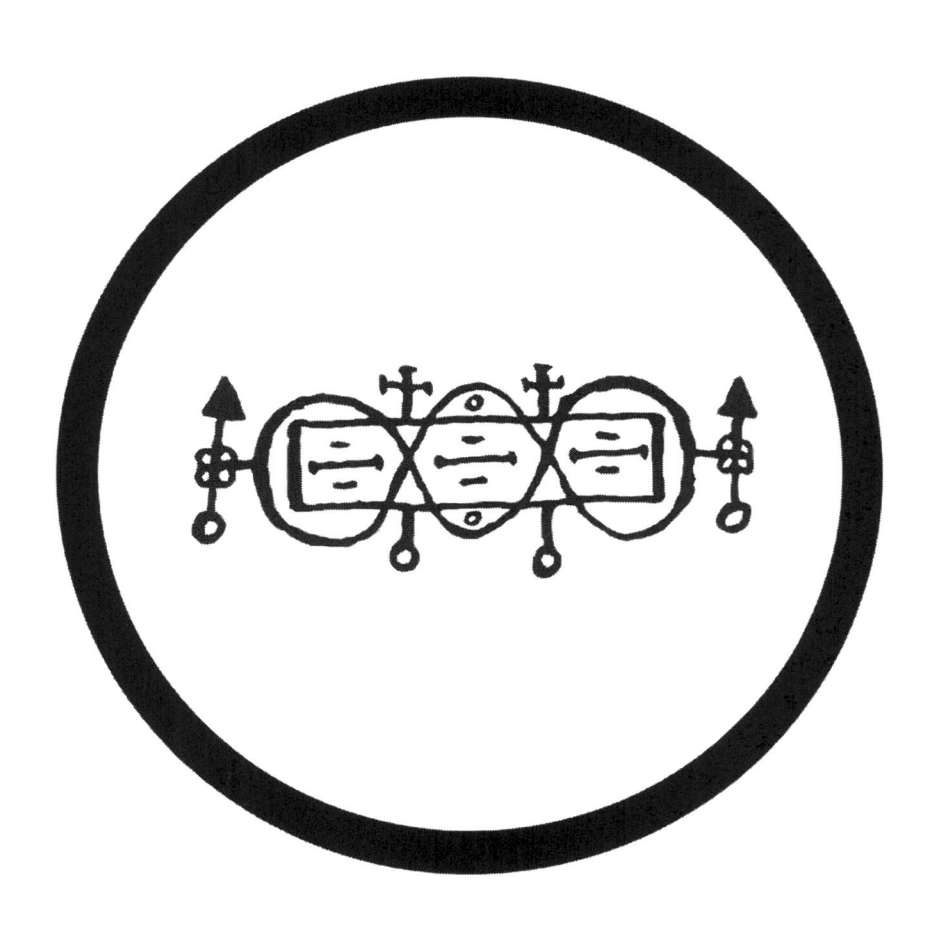

White cloth stained with blood.
The sound of a waterfall.
The smell of a stagnant pond.
A pale blue sky with a bright full moon.

31. Foras

Age well. It's easiest to perform magick when there's a problem that needs solving, but there are powers you can use now, which you'll appreciate later. Call on Foras to make you age well, and you will appear young and energetic as you age, with people believing you are much younger than you appear to be. You can perform this ritual once and allow it to work in the decades that follow.

Fascinate the jaded. If somebody has become bored by you or feels you are no longer as exciting or interesting as you once were, this power can give you an air of mysterious excitement that will make you fascinating. A friend, lover, or even a business partner, will once again be intrigued and attracted to your presence and your thoughts.

Understand a loved one. If you are serious about a relationship, it helps to understand the other person's deeper needs. This power works by making the other person more expressive while helping you to perceive the true needs expressed behind anything that is spoken. It can be used at any time but is useful in the early stages of a relationship when you are deciding if you want to meet those needs, and also after years have passed, when needs have changed. Many relationships fail because people don't check up on changing needs and if you want a relationship to survive, this perception can help.

The Sigil of Foras

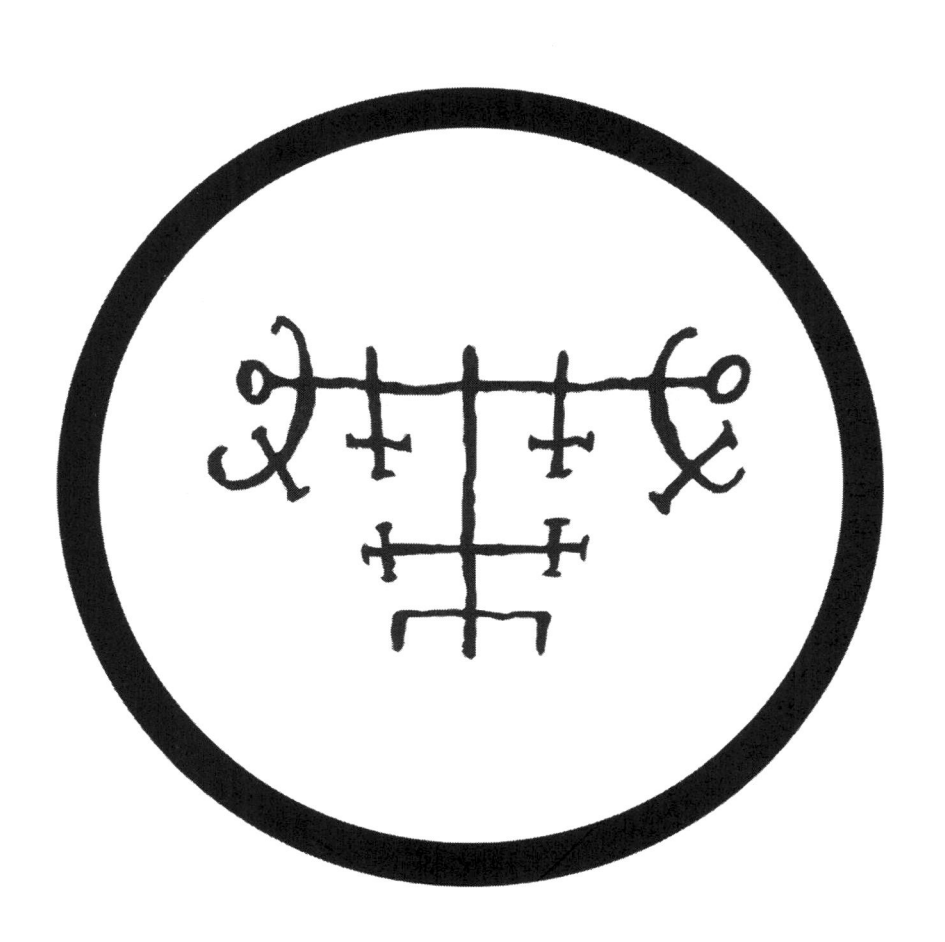

Stars are visible through the clouds.
Birdsong.
The scent of a rose.
Grey clouds touched by golden light.

32. Asmodai

The will to decide. Making a decision can be unexpectedly difficult. Feelings of uncertainty and fear can get in the way of your ability to make important decisions. This power will improve your ability to access the willpower to make a decision. The power can also improve your intuition when it comes to major decisions, so you've got more chance of making the right decision.

Develop a skill. If you've worked on a skill for any length of time and found that your ability has plateaued, this power can help you find new heights of ability. Don't be surprised if you are led to find new teachers, as that is often the easiest way to get better. You may find that, without changing anything at all, you get better, but be open to the possibility of researching and testing new methods to improve your skills.

Conceal the valuable. If there's a valuable painting on your wall, or a safe, a precious heirloom, or any object of importance, you can use this power to make it effectively invisible to any who would steal it.

The Sigil of Asmodai

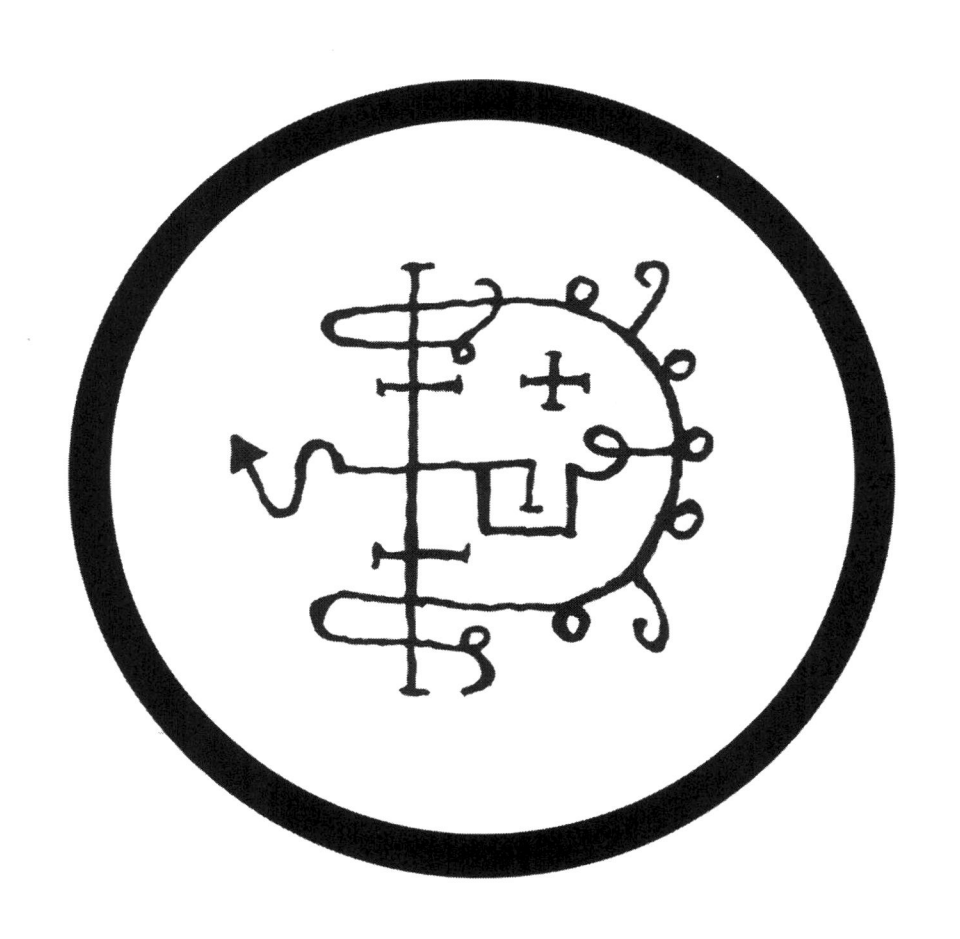

A silhouetted bull against a crimson sunset.
The sound of many people breathing in sleep.
The smell of hot iron.
In a deep blue sky, the red sun.

33. Gaap

Bring drowsiness. This is a minor curse but the effects can last long enough to weaken a person enough to give you an advantage over them. It causes constant yawning, drowsiness and foggy thoughts.

Create arguments. The basis of this power is hatred, and it will cause people to see the worst in each other. It can be used against a group, or against two people. In some cases, you might choose to make one person hateful while leaving the other untouched. It's a creative way to create conflict because the hatred of one person is so disorienting for the other.

Irrational Lust. This creates a lust in the target that is unstable, inconsistent, and disturbing to the person experiencing it. The person they lust after may not be you, so this is not used for seduction. It is used to make somebody act out of character in a way that may be destabilising, confusing, and harmful to reputation and relationships.

The Sigil of Gaap

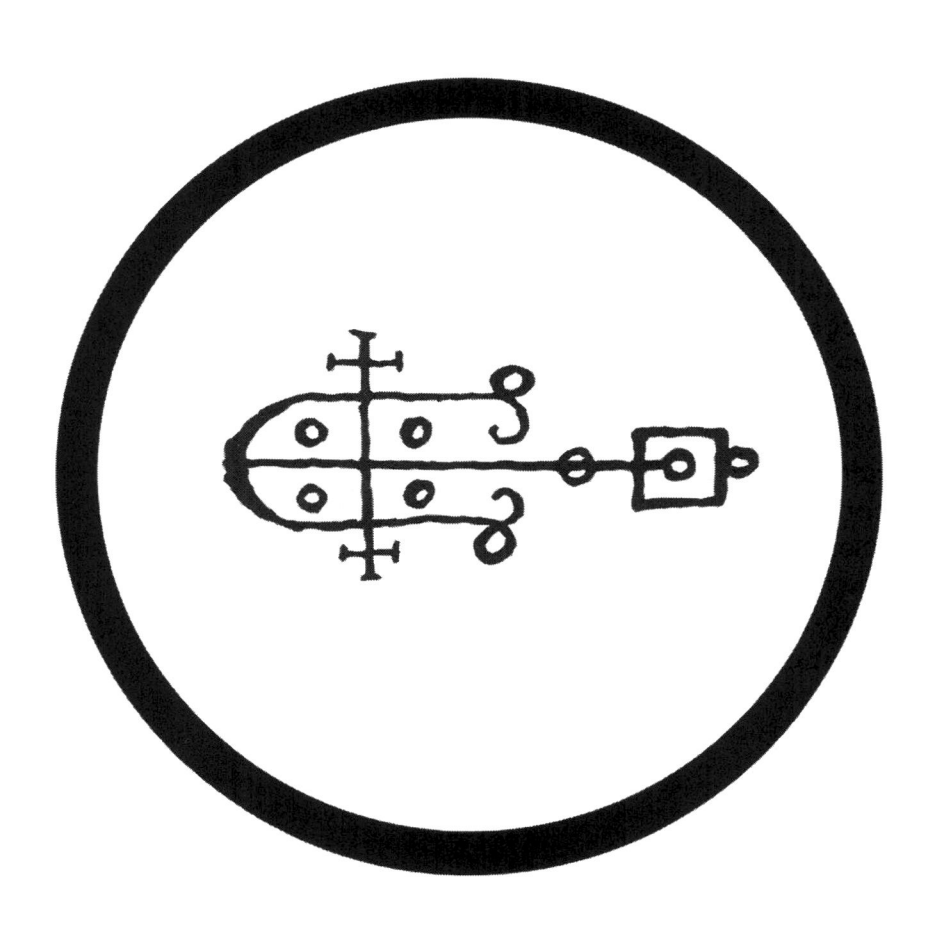

Dead grass trampled into the mud.
The sound of many hissing snakes.
The smell of freshly dug soil.
Grey clouds touched by pink light.

34. Furfur

Anger the calm. When somebody is normally calm under all circumstances, you can make the person become angry. This has the effect of confusing the person's self-image, as well as leading to strained relationships, and mistakes at work. Avoid using this on somebody close to you, or when you could become the victim of the anger.

Cause electrical storms. I like this power because it's great for making electronic equipment malfunction. It can even be used on cars or other machines if they have electrical components. Although the power describes electrical storms, I have never had the need to create a storm. It may work, it may not, but unless you have a real need, I don't know why you'd try. If you want to harm another person, a surge of electrical disruption can damage or disable equipment. In modern times, this is more disruptive to most people than an actual storm, making it a useful curse. You can specify the equipment or ask that all the electrical equipment used by a person or organisation is subject to failure. You do not need to tell the demon to create an electrical storm within the equipment; you only need to know that you are directing the demon to damage electrical equipment. Although the application is modern, the demon has no problem understanding what you mean. Curiously, the power will sometimes cause problems with a target's software rather than the equipment itself.

Investigate in secret. When you want to snoop around in somebody else's private life or business affairs, you are taking a risk, but your investigations are less likely to be revealed if you call for the cloak of secrecy that this power can bring.

The Sigil of Furfur

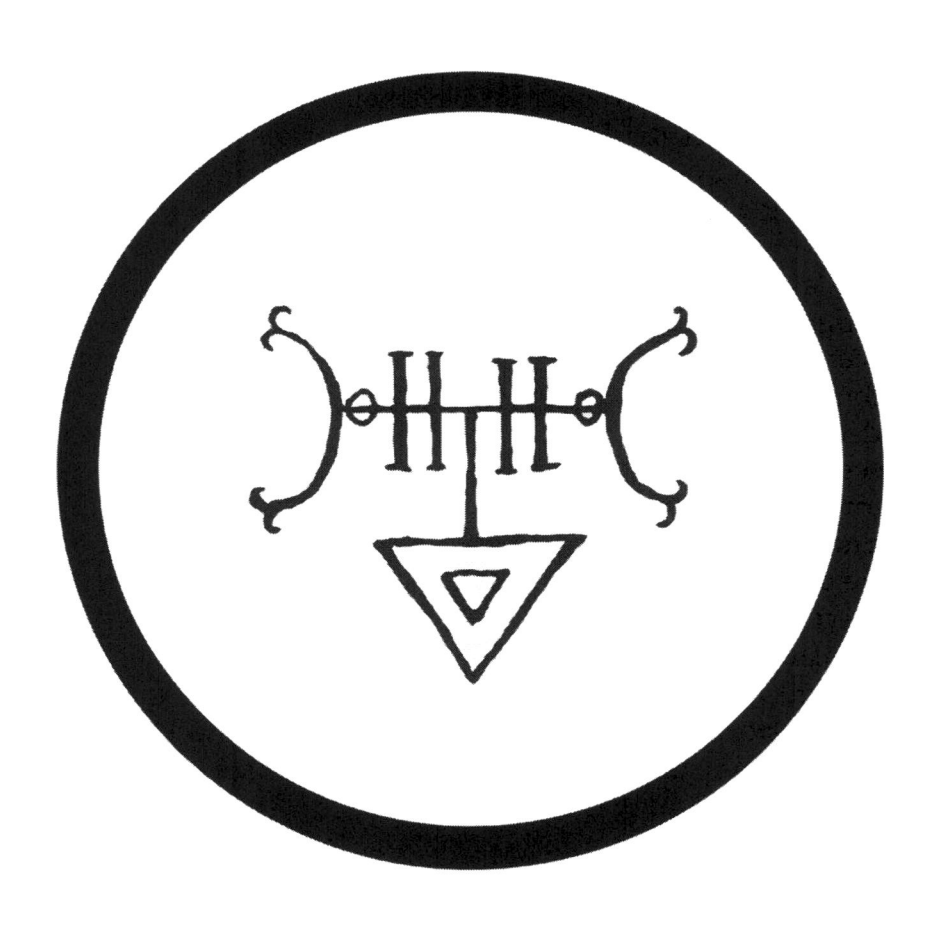

A smoking bonfire of drenched tree branches.
The sound of metal being hammered.
The odour of mould.
A blue sky warms to yellow as a white sun rises.

35. Marchosias

Negotiate forcefully. Most of the time it's good to negotiate calmly, to keep everybody open to your ideas. Sometimes, when peaceful negotiations don't bring results, you want to show strength. This does not mean you become a bully, but that the force of your intent is made clear. It is about power, not anger, and if you sense that it could help when somebody is stubborn, or even indecisive, it can move negotiations forward.

Support entrepreneurship. If you are trying to create wealth or even earn a living as an entrepreneur, the demon will support your efforts. For the self-employed, this means that the demon blesses and empowers all your actions, offering guidance and wisdom as you work. It is worth repeating this ritual every few months because it is likely that your work will develop, and your needs change. You ask for general support rather than for specific solutions, and the demon will bring more success to your work.

Dissuade an enemy. If you have an enemy, this power will make them fear you to the point that they no longer want to risk harming you in any way.

The Sigil of Marchosias

Ashes and snow drift from a slab of black rock.
The sound of metal being hammered.
The taste of smoke.
From a russet darkness grows a dim red light.

36. Stolas

Relieve pain. For pain that lingers in old wounds, or that has been with you for a long time without a clear cause, this power can bring relief.

Obtain a creative breakthrough. Breakthroughs don't happen on the first day of creative work, so use this power when you feel you have been working long enough to be ready for a breakthrough. You can also use it when you've gone way beyond that time, and feel uninspired or tired of a project.

The Sigil of Stolas

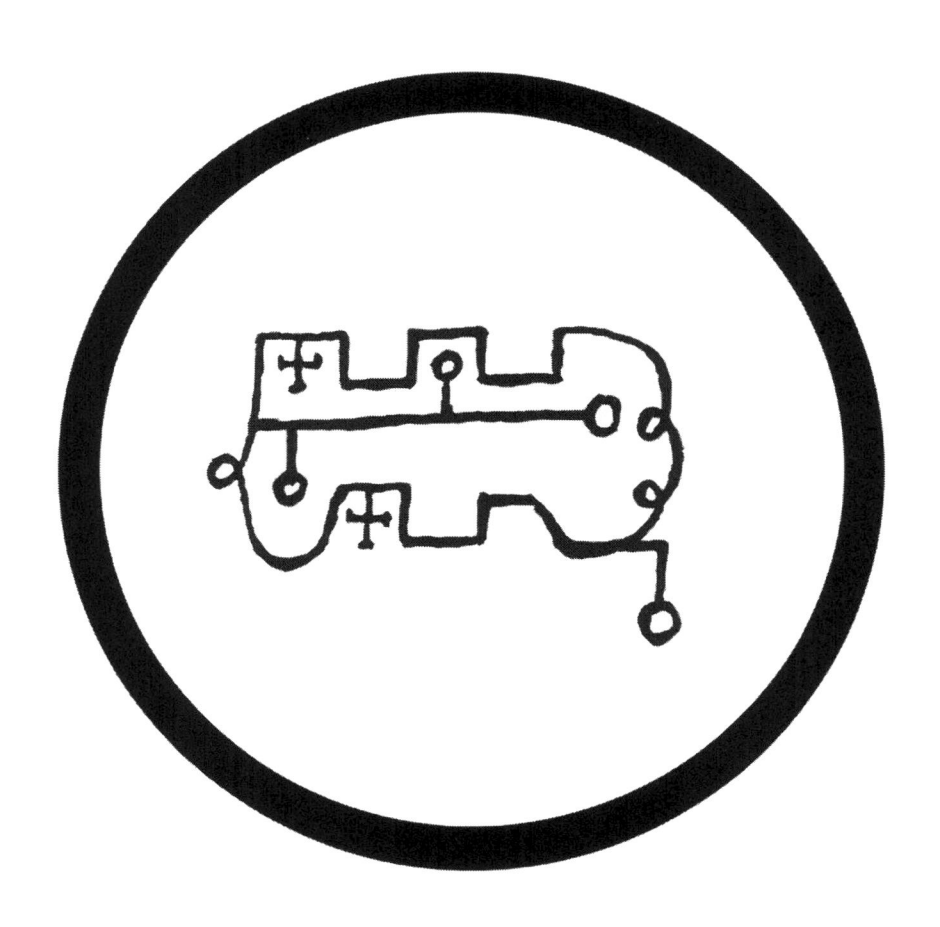

A golden human skull on a slab of black marble.
The sound of a waterfall.
The odour of mould.
A black sky is filled with brilliant blue stars.

37. Phenix

Easy conversation. If you feel uneasy in social settings, this power can help you speak with ease. It will also encourage you to listen well, which is an attractive quality and an important part of conversation.

Subjugate the disruptive. This power will make any person quieter for a few weeks, and can be used against loud neighbours, an angry person in your family, or any other person you wish to subjugate for a time.

Improve musical composition. If you write music you will find it easier to write with ease and inspiration if you ask the demon to support your efforts.

Make writing persuasive. Whether you're writing a blog post or a love letter, you can ask the demon to make you more persuasive.

The Sigil of Phenix

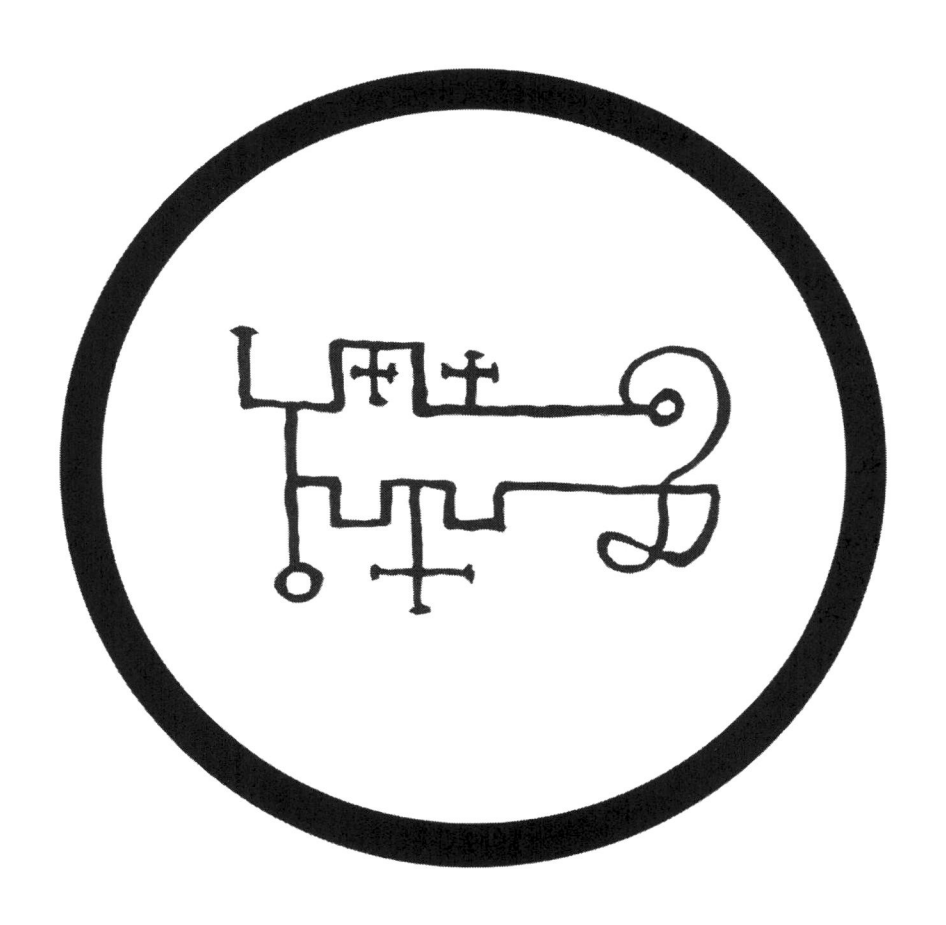

A red rosebud frozen in glassy ice.
The sound of a waterfall.
The smell of tart fruit, like berries.
A white sky becomes glittering amber.

38. Halphas

Clarity regarding ambition. When you have an ambition, you need to obtain clarity on how far away your goals are, and the steps required to achieve them. Ask the demon to let you see the reality of your ambition and how it can be achieved. You may obtain an immediate vision, or you may gain a more subtle understanding in the days that follow the ritual.

Develop important skills. When you know that certain skills are important to obtaining a goal, this power can help you develop those skills with speed.

Advance within an organisation. I have heard people refer to this as a power for obtaining a promotion, but I believe it is more about gradually gaining power within an organisation. You let the demon know that you have a specific goal, higher up within the organisation, and as you work toward that goal the demon will support your efforts.

Fortune in leadership. When you lead other people, in any situation from a social group to a business, or even within the military, this power makes your role as a leader more productive.

The Sigil of Halphas

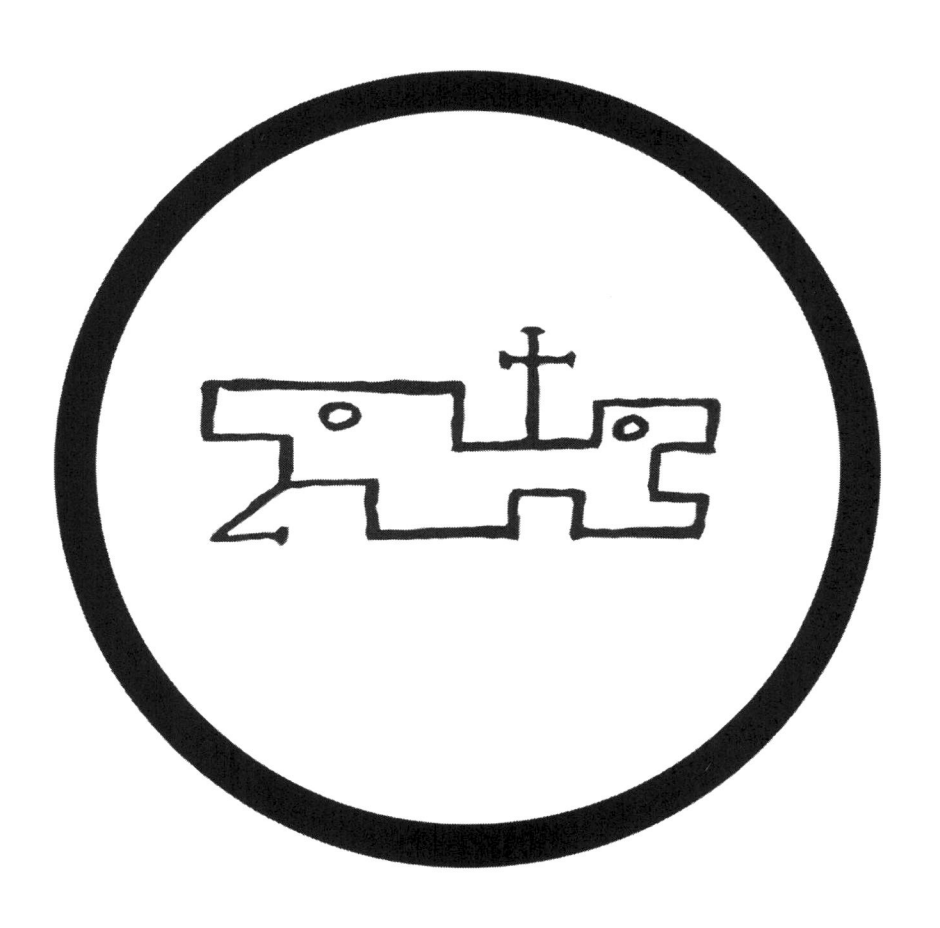

A circle of wet pebbles in a dry, empty field.
The sound of wind rushing through bare trees.
The scent of a rose.
From a green darkness grows a bright red light.

39. Malphas

Discover allies. People who do well in the world usually do so with the support of other people. When you know what you want, call on this power to help you discover those who share and support your goals.

Placate the competition. When you are in competition with somebody, either in sport, the arts, or business, this power can make the other competitor feel a peaceful calm that dulls their competitive edge.

The Sigil of Malphas

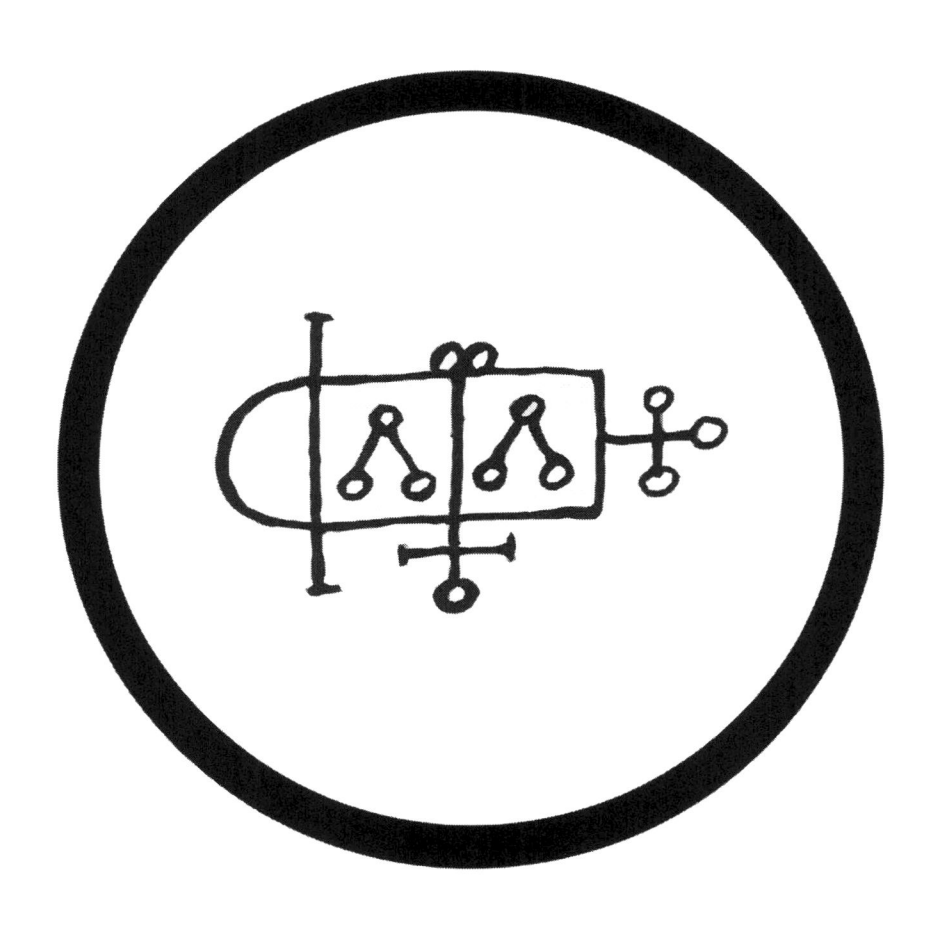

A black tree laden with red fruit.
The angry barking of many dogs.
The smell of burning wood.
From a blue darkness grows a dim green light.

40. Raum

Curse for vengeance. Ask the demon to make somebody suffer a hurtful loss. This power will bring intense suffering to the person who experiences the loss, so be certain you can be at peace with their pain.

Cause mistrust. This curses your target so that they are mistrusted by all who come into contact with them. The effects last many weeks and can seriously damage a person's life.

The Sigil of Raum

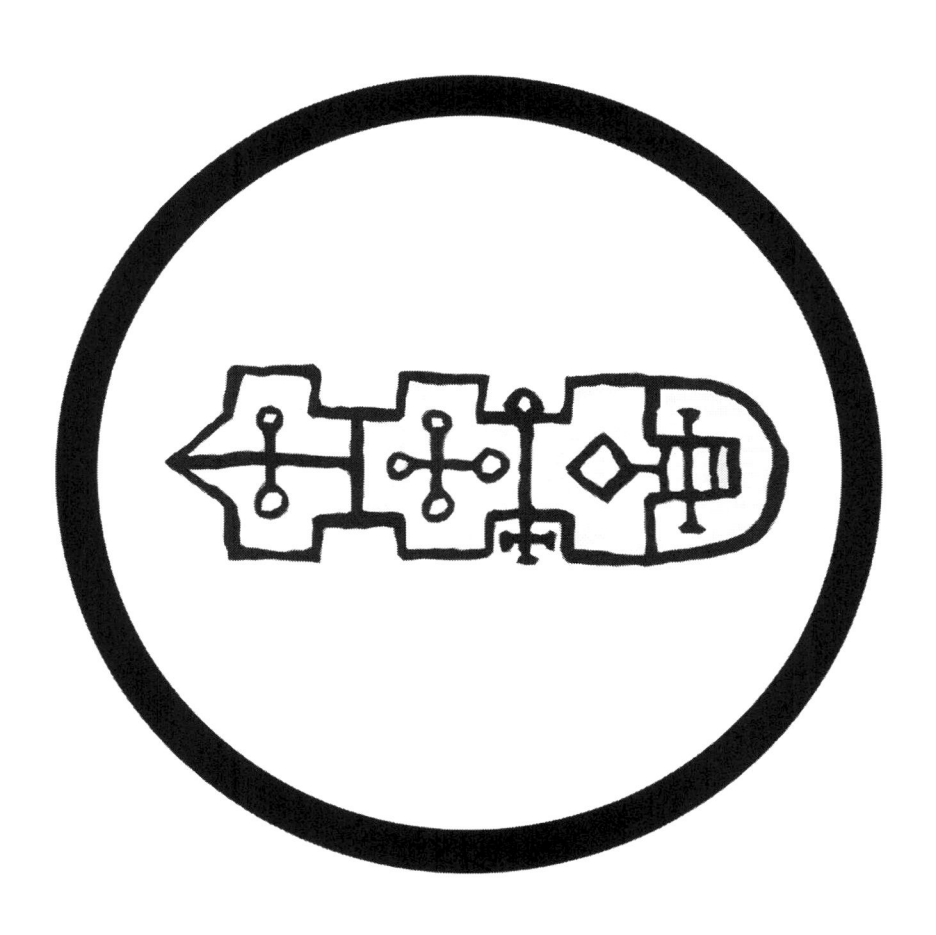

The bones of a horse on the black mud of a dried lake.
The sound of many feet on stone.
The taste of blood.
The black sky becomes light with sickly yellow clouds.

41. Forcalor

Persistent sickness. When somebody is unwell this power makes them remain unwell. It does not worsen their condition but makes them remain unwell for longer.

Business failure. Call on the demon to make a business fail. You get the best results when the business knows of you and is in competition with you, or when you are close to somebody who is important in that business.

Endanger another. This power makes a person more likely to have accidents that can lead to severe injury.

Protection from magick. Call for protection from magick that has been designed to harm you. This is most effective when you know somebody is trying to harm you. If you know who that person is, it is even more effective.

The Sigil of Forcalor

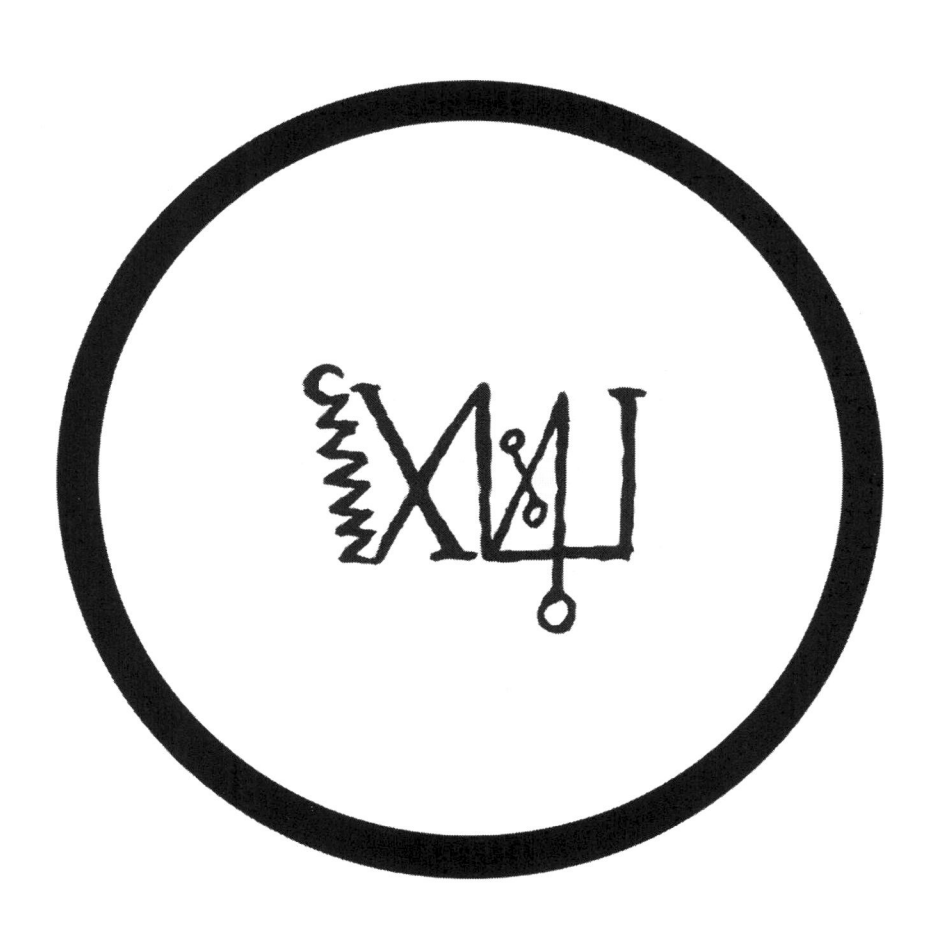

Moonlight through mist over a field of rocks.
The sound of metal being hammered.
The smell of freshly dug soil.
A dark blue sky with a golden sun.

42. Vepar

Travel safely. Safe travel occurs when you have the strength and energy to make the journey with confidence, and this is the power that the demon will give you. Instead of asking for safe travel, ask for the strength and energy to travel safely.

Subdue the proud. This is a minor curse to make a proud person less boastful, or even to experience self-doubt and shame.

Infect to make weak. This will cause a person to become infected with a short-term illness that makes them weak.

Increase sickness. When somebody is already unwell, use this power to prevent recovery and make their symptoms worsen.

The Sigil of Vepar

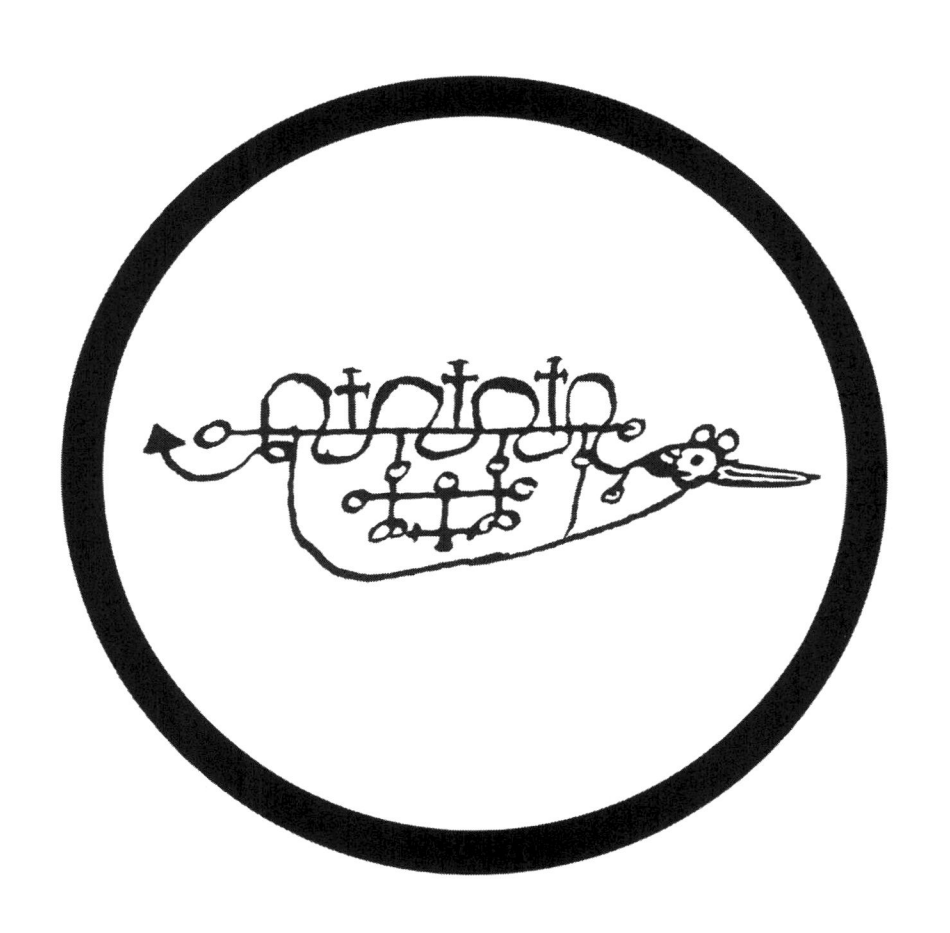

A pregnant young woman holding a dead crow.
The sound of many feet on gravel.
The taste of charcoal.
A yellow sky fades to grey as the white sun rises.

43. Sabnock

Exhaust another. There are many creative uses for this power, and it makes your target suffer from mounting exhaustion. The more they fight to overcome the exhaustion through willpower, the worse they feel. Only when they seek recuperation through rest will they overcome the exhaustion. You may have achieved all that you set out to achieve, but if not, repeat the ritual to bring the exhaustion back. This can be one of the most effective ways to weaken somebody or disrupt their life, but some people handle exhaustion better than others. If your target is still apparently strong two weeks after you perform the ritual, you may wish to add other curses or rituals to enrich the attack.

Cause delusions. The delusions brought on by this demon are based on the concept of intrusion. The person you attack will feel as though their mind or body is being invaded by thoughts, sensations, disease, and even parasites. This is most effective against people with no knowledge of the occult. An occultist would probably recognise these as symptoms of an attack and would put up an appropriate defence.

The Sigil of Sabnock

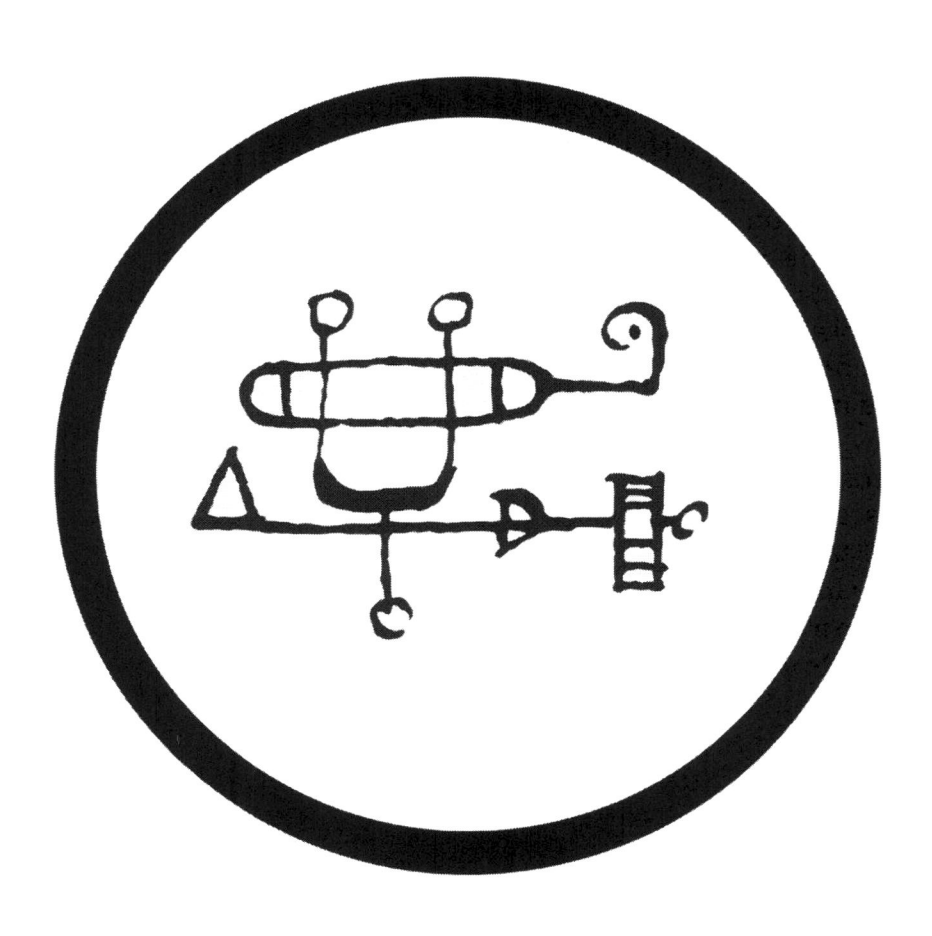

A broken white boulder on black soil.
The sound of lustful moaning, as from a drowsy orgy.
The taste of charcoal.
A dim white sun behind a sheet of grey cloud.

44. Shax

Disturb plans. With this power, you can make somebody else develop plans that fail. It can be guided at an individual or a group of people within an organisation. It can be used to harm enemies or to gain an advantage over competitors.

Put an enemy off guard. Although this power can be used against a direct enemy, so that they do not sense you are working to harm them, it is also invaluable when used against a competitor. Make a competitor assume you are no threat and they will be unprepared for your next move. It also makes them less competitive, and less likely to develop their work or business, so that as you develop and grow your business, you are always going to be ahead. You can use this power once and get a strong and lasting result, but if you sense that the competitor has resumed work, repeat the ritual. If you have many competitors, you can direct the ritual at all of them at once, but it is best if you work against those who truly compete with you, and not at everybody who works in the same area or industry.

The Sigil of Shax

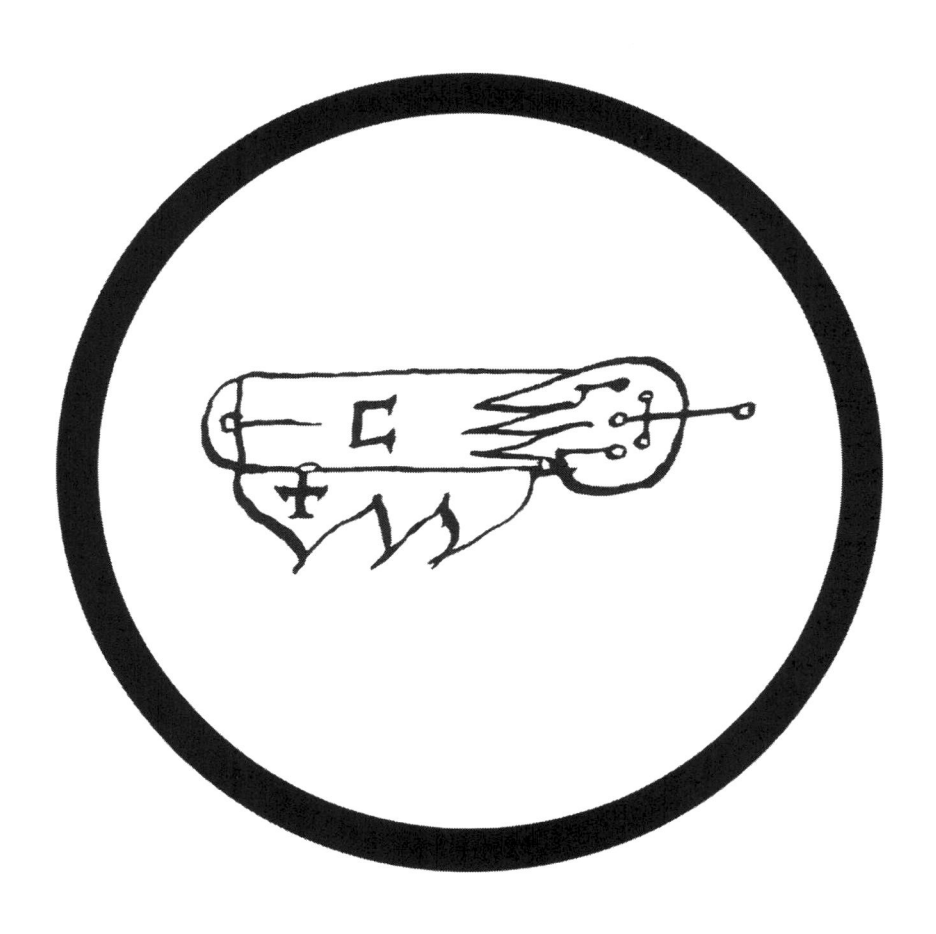

A black human skull on a slab of white marble.
The sound of lustful moaning, as from a drowsy orgy.
The smell of a stagnant pond.
A white sky becomes a dark, cloudy blue.

45. Vine

Create confusing emotions. This power will make somebody who once loved you, love you again, but this is not a ritual of reconciliation. It is used to make somebody weak when you are going through a divorce, or if a former lover is aggressive or accusatory. It will make that person feel love and compassion for you. This does not create any desire for reconciliation but produces sympathy, empathy, and a desire to make your life good. When a former lover is causing problems, it can be a powerful way to gain an advantage.

Magickal focus. If you find that you lack concentration when practicing magick, use this power to improve your abilities. It's useful if you're working on more complex magickal skills such as evocation.

Discover disloyal thieves. Many people can attack you and your work, and many people can steal from you. This power is designed to seek out those who appear loyal, but who have stolen from you. In business, most theft that I have witnessed has not been made by random employees, but by the trusted friends of those in power. Whatever the scale of your work or business, if you suspect theft or disloyalty of any kind, the demon will make you aware of the culprit and how they are operating.

Break the will of mercenaries. The word 'mercenaries' makes you think about hired guns, but I'm talking about people hired, paid, or otherwise compensated for working to defeat or harm you. They may be private detectives, lawyers, racketeers, occultists, or everyday thugs. The demon will seek out anybody who is hired to work against you and will break their will, filling them with fear. They will cease their efforts.

The Sigil of Vine

Black thorns gleaming with frost.
The sound of laboured breathing.
The smell of a stagnant pond.
A pale yellow sunset with a bright full moon.

46. Bifrons

Superior plans. When you need a better plan than your opponent, this power will give you that plan. It works when preparing for a legal battle as well as it works when trying to defeat a competitor.

Speak with the dead. In your request, name the person you wish to speak to again. After the ritual, focus on your memories of them right through to the last time you met, and then allow yourself to sit quietly. You may sense words or emotions, immediately or in the days to come. You may have actual conversations (with the words heard in your mind, or sometimes out loud) that appear to be real. Despite the apparent potential of this power I have found it inconsistent, and remain unconvinced that I am actually speaking with the dead. It may be a complex illusion. The comfort brought, and the insights given, are useful but you may find you are left with doubts about the authentic connection. We do not know what happens after death, and it is possible this power only allows us to commune with the soul of the person when they were alive, reaching back in time to connect with their subconscious. Or it could be we *are* speaking with the dead. Form your own opinion based on results.

Remember your past. Reminiscing for the sake of nostalgia is often amusing, but this power is about reaching for half-sensed memories that concern you. If you don't know what that means, you have no need for this power. If you are troubled by half-remembered incidents and wish to recall them, use this power, and let the memories return. They may do so in a moment of clear recall, or with a gathering sense of clarity as you gently reminisce. Do not try to force memories, because they only ever elude you when chased. Allow them to return and they will.

The Sigil of Bifrons

A black dog, its fur wet with blood.
The sound of many hissing snakes.
The scent of animal fur.
Black clouds touched by blue light.

47. Vuall

Restore trust. When trust has been lost, whether through your actions or because of another person's own problems with trust, this power can restore trust. It can be directed at one person, or a group, and will make them believe you are trustworthy. The deceptive can use this to gain the upper hand and commit acts that go undetected. You can also use it to bring authentic trust to a valued relationship.

Improved orgasm. This power is often described as bringing more sensuality to a relationship, but the more honest description is that it improves orgasm for both partners. If you don't have a regular partner, it makes you more likely to achieve satisfaction for yourself and any lover you spend time with. Use this once, and your connection to orgasm can be changed for life. Only repeat if there is a noticeable reduction in pleasure.

Fascinate strangers. It takes confidence to talk to strangers, and this power won't help you with that, but if you do spend time with people you've never met before, there is more chance that they will be fascinated by you in a way that causes sexual arousal. The effects last for some weeks.

Sense a relationship. If you want to sense how a relationship might develop, use this power. It can be used before a relationship is happening, or when you have been with somebody for years. It lets you sense what the future holds. Nothing in the future is stable so this only shows you the most likely future, and you can act on what you sense, to change the future. You will gain a sense of the future through flashes of insight especially when you are talking to the person, and this may go on for some days or even weeks, after the ritual.

The Sigil of Vuall

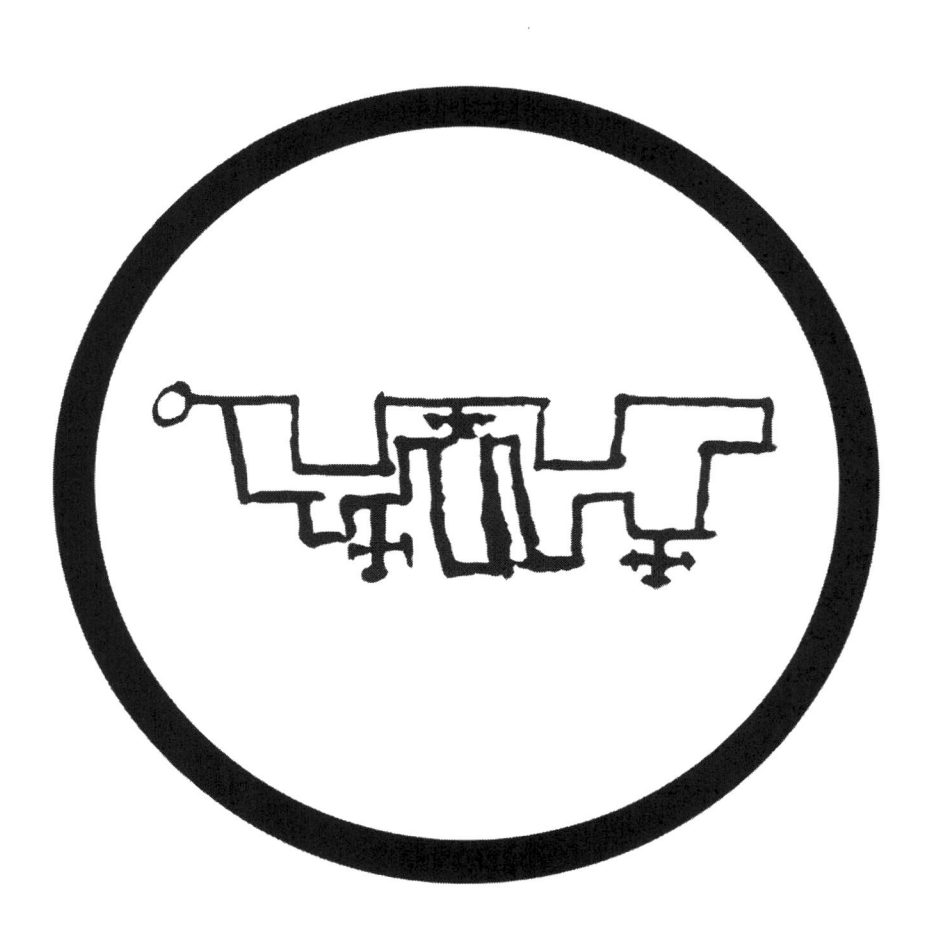

White petals surround a black stone.
The sound of many hissing snakes.
The scent of animal fur.
Distant lightning in a clear blue sky.

48. Haagenti

Personal change. It could be said that Haagenti has one power, and it is the power to bring about change in yourself. The other two powers listed below are perhaps subsets of this power. The demon can be called to help you change any aspect of your personality or outlook that you wish to change. If you feel you are too angry, judgemental, lazy or boring, you can call on the demon to let the negative aspect fall away and be replaced with a positive one.

Remove fear. A strong way to change yourself is to remove fear when it obstructs you. If fear is making you live weakly, cowering from experience or the next step you know you should take, this power can remove fear. Some have reported that this can also help with general and social anxiety, by making you more confident. Confidence is the removal of fear.

Break habits. If you put effort into breaking a habit or addiction, this power will multiply the effectiveness of your effort. Magick will never break a habit for you. The hard work is still yours to do, but this can make it bearable and can even give you the wisdom to find techniques and alternatives to the habit that enable you to make a clean break.

The Sigil of Haagenti

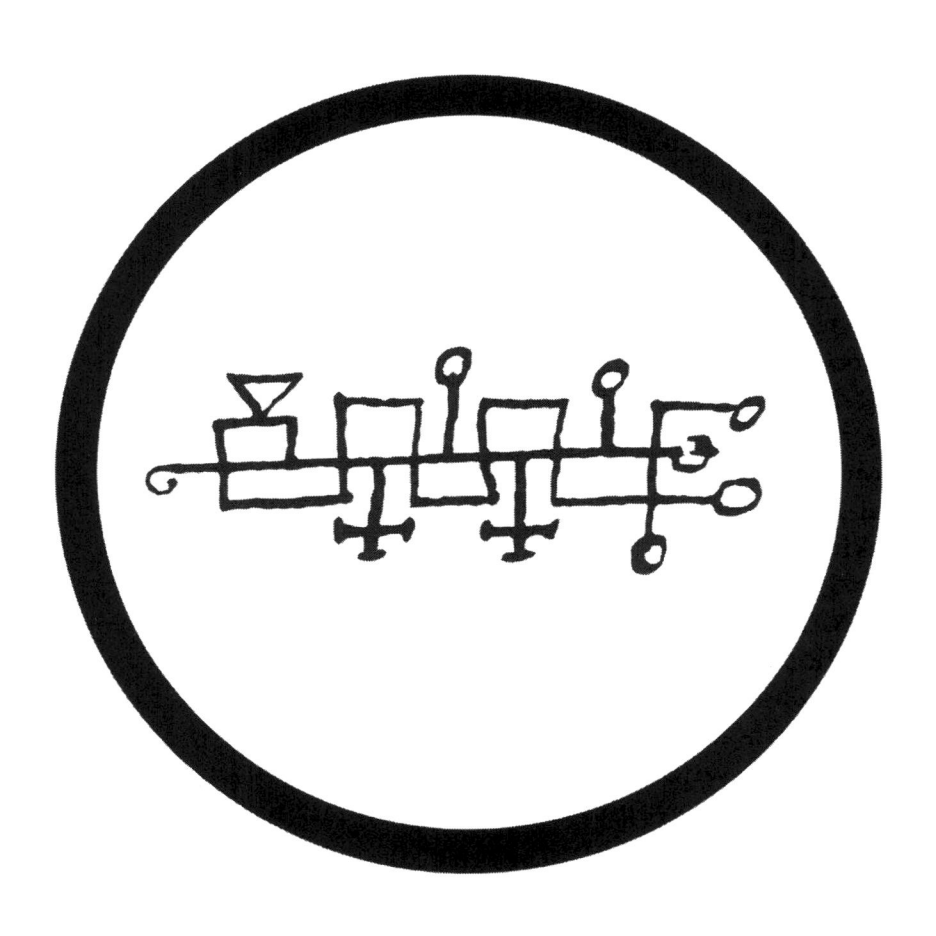

A muddy pond, its surface scattered with dead insects.
The sound of many people breathing in sleep.
The taste of honey.
The black sky becomes misty with reddish clouds.

49. Crocell

Encourage lust. Make another person desire you in a sexual way. If there is any potential for lust, the person you desire will desire you in return. If there is no potential, this cannot seduce somebody to want you against their will. If there is strong desire, it may cause the other person to act on their lust, but if you use the ritual on a quiet, reserved person, or somebody in a committed relationship, it may take some careful work to determine if lust is present. If the ritual has worked, you will usually sense it clearly, and any attempt to flirt or connect with the other person will be met with a positive reaction. This even works in a relationship when lust has calmed too much.

Understand magick. This power is about gaining an insight into magick as you read. If you read magick books, use this power to get the most out of them.

Improve learning. When studying for a short period of time, this power will help you take in and understand more information than usual. Especially useful in preparation for an exam.

Hypnotic charm. If you talk to somebody who rarely yields to your decisions or desires, whether at work or at home, this power makes you gently persuasive so that all resistance and energy leaves the other person and they are convinced by your words. Use it generally to make a person be convinced by you at all times, or direct it at one decision you want the other person to make, and then work your charm through conversation.

The Sigil of Crocell

A young man holds two daggers in his outstretched arms.
Birdsong.
The scent of a distant storm.
The black sky lightens to pale blue.

50. Furcas

For supernatural ability. If you use divination, seek visions, or attempt anything that might be called supernatural, including astral projection, this power can improve your ability to connect with your natural talent. It will only have an effect if you are working to develop such an ability and will have no effect if you just want to be more psychic. If you want to be more psychic, choose a method that is known to work, and then ask the demon to improve your ability to learn. If you already possess a supernatural ability of any kind, you can reach your full potential with it more rapidly by calling for the demon's aid.

For intuition. While intuition can be seen as a blending of personal wisdom and supernatural abilities, it is listed separately from the above power because it will work even if you aren't actively developing your intuition. The only effort you need to make is an attempt to trust your feelings, and heed intuition when it occurs.

Bring guilt. This power makes somebody feel the level of guilt they deserve to feel, from your perspective. I have found it can be used to make a person feel guilty about any action they have taken. If you don't know what actions they have taken, you can ask for the demon to seek out their darkest guilt and they will then be plagued by that guilt. You may use this for revenge or to urge somebody to change their ways.

Stir hatred. Hatred can be used to distract, to end relationships, or cause chaos in an organization. Be cautious about where you use this, because if the person you charge with hatred is in your vicinity, the experience may not be pleasant. You can stir hatred in one person, or make two people hate each other.

The Sigil of Furcas

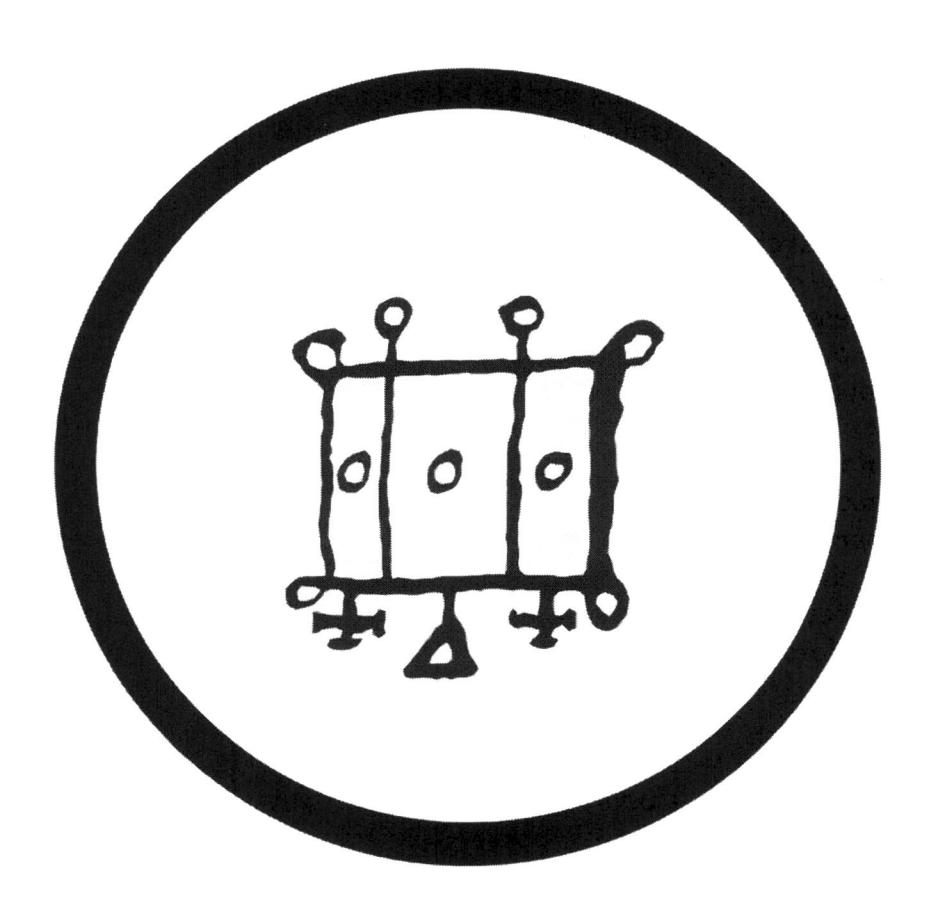

In bright sunlight, a muddy river is streaked with blood.
Birdsong.
The smell of burnt hair.
A dark blue sky becomes pale blue as a yellow sun rises.

51. Balam

Reduce attention. When somebody is bothering you with aggression, unwanted attention, or intrusive questions, this will reduce their intention to be near you or to investigate you.

Reduced presence. Use this power to make your actions go unnoticed by all. You should make it clear what you are trying to hide, or the demon will make you go unnoticed by everybody in all matters. When you are working on something that needs to remain unseen, over a short period of time, this power will make you unnoticed. You might use this for a single night of clandestine investigation, or for a few weeks of activity, but it is not meant to protect or conceal something for much longer than that.

Be convincing. This power can make you convincing when trying to defuse a situation, or appear innocent (whether you are or not) when talking to an accuser. Use the ritual in advance of any potential problem. Most people wait until they are about to go to court to use a ritual like this because there is no pressing need, but if you use it when there is no problem, you may avoid ever ending up in court. And you should take on this power permanently. This is not a ritual that needs to be repeated because the demon bestows the skill to you, and once learned it is learned.

The Sigil of Balam

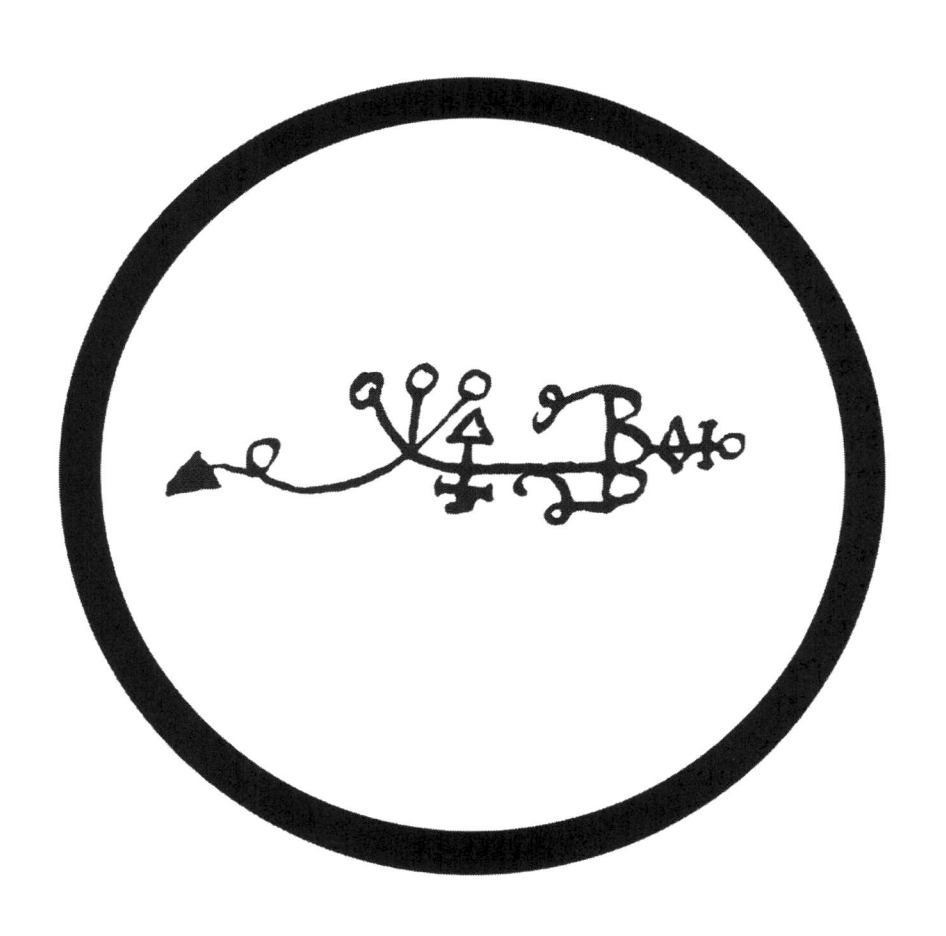

An eagle overhead in a clear blue sky.
The sound of many feet on gravel.
The smell of hot iron.
Blue-white lightning in a grey sky.

52. Alloces

Perceive the future. Ask the demon to open your perception so that you can see the future. This is not a general form of divination but is used when you seek one definite answer about what will actually happen. Sometimes you use divination to find the most likely outcome, and then work to change that outcome. With this power, you are asking what will actually happen so you can plan your response. This is best used when you are trying to guess the plans of an enemy or competitor. What will they actually do, and what will you have to face? Answers can be given that cover a few days or several years. The short-term answers are the most accurate. If you get a direct response from the demon, in the form of images, whispers, or sensations, that is a result that feels satisfying and accurate, but more often you will notice an emergent impression of what the future holds in the days following the ritual, usually when you are not thinking about the problem. Go for a walk, think about nothing, and that's one of the best ways to allow answers to arise.

Perceive hidden truth. When the truth you seek is based on emotions rather than facts, use this power. It helps you know what somebody really feels about you, about a situation, or about something secret. The sensation may be immediate or may become clear when you interact with that person.

Bind the harmful. When you want to stop somebody from harming you, binding them is a strong form of magick. It can be better than a curse because it prevents that person from even thinking about harming you. It's also good to use on somebody when you're not sure that they're an enemy. You may suspect that somebody has bad intention, but you don't want to curse somebody based on a hunch, so bind them and avoid the problem ever developing.

The Sigil of Alloces

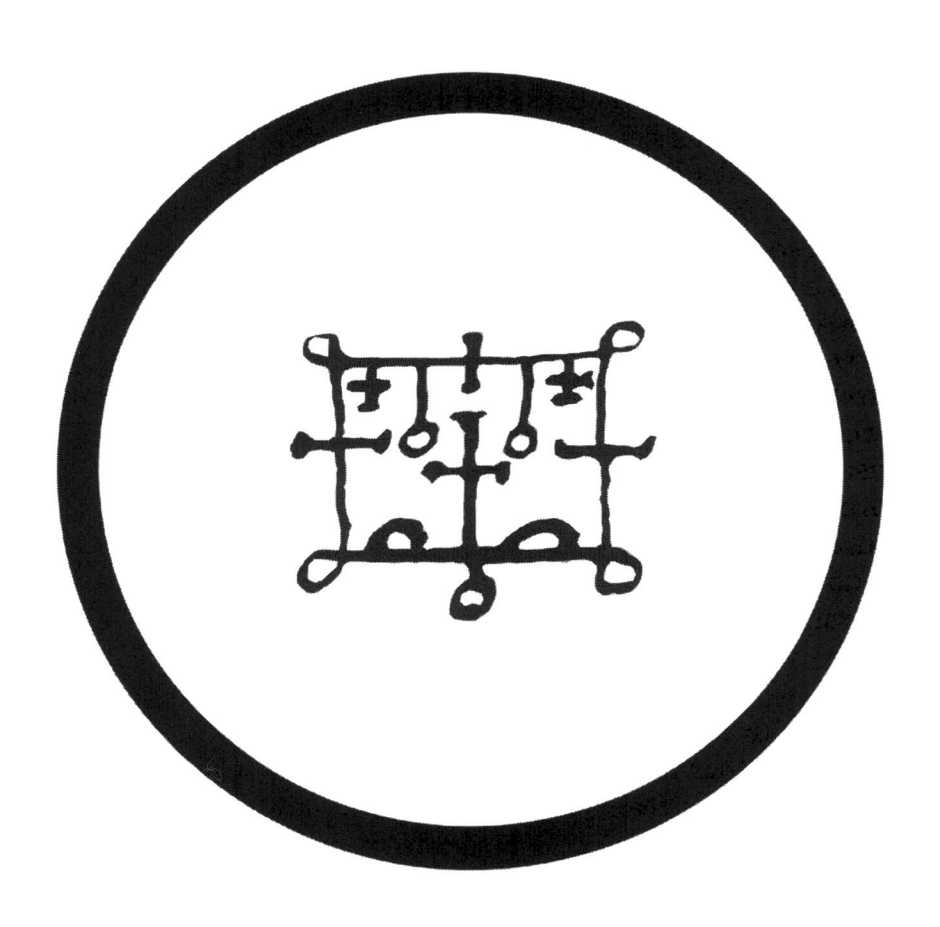

In the blue light of dawn, a blackened forest smokes.
The sound of many feet on gravel.
The smell of hot iron.
In a deep blue sky, a red full moon.

53. Caim

Weaken another. You can use this power to make another person feel weak and helpless when they are in your company. This is extremely powerful. You can also use the power to make any person you know become weak when they attempt to attack, undermine, or question your decisions.

Communicate clearly. Even when you are good at communicating with people, in groups or one on one, there are times when communication becomes difficult due to a variety of issues. It may be that you are trying to communicate with somebody who lacks empathy, understanding, or intelligence, or people who are trapped in habitual thoughts or a resistance to change. When communication dries up, use this power to add energy to your communication (whether written or spoken) that will make it understood by your intended audience.

The Sigil of Caim

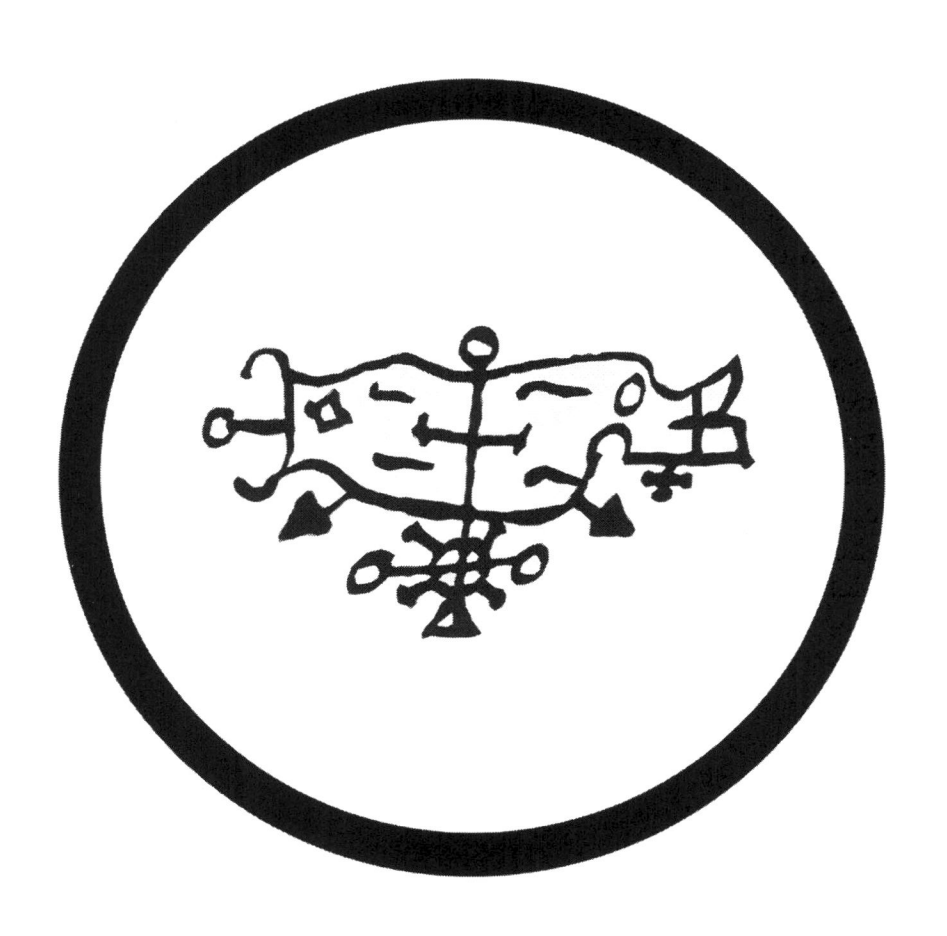

A jawbone in watery mud.
The sound of laboured breathing.
The odour of mould.
Blue-grey clouds touched by amber light.

54. Murmus

Calm thought. When a problem feels like it's taking over your life, it's almost impossible to find perspective or get into a mental space that is flexible and creative, because fear freezes thought. If you require the ability to think calmly, during a crisis or when faced with an overwhelming problem, this power can give you the mental clarity you require to find a solution.

Remove unwanted energy.
Use this power to clear any space, whether a home, garden, or somewhere you work, of energies that don't feel right. You might perceive this as a haunting or poltergeist activity, or something more directed like a curse. Whatever you sense, this power can cleanse and clear the location.

Urge caution. When you know somebody is heading for a disaster, you can use this power to make them more cautious. If somebody is ambitious, you can use this to lessen their ambition, as a form of attack or punishment. When directed at a friend, you use it when you're certain you know better. Like those times when a friend is about to sign up to a mortgage you know they can't afford, and you don't want to see them go under. Use this power to make your friend think things through with intelligence rather than making emotional decisions. This can be a great gift.

Trap in cycles of thought. This power is used to make an enemy or competitor becomes stuck in a cycle of repetitive thoughts with ongoing indecision. It can be used to frustrate plans and gain an advantage over that person.

The Sigil of Murmus

A tree of pink blossom on a barren, black hillside.
The sound of metal being hammered.
A smell like wet straw.
A pale grey sky with a golden sun.

55. Orobas

Improve divination. If you use any form of divination, even if it's a form you've made up yourself, this power works to improve your ability to work that magick of divination and also to interpret what you learn more honestly and insightfully.

Improve your image. Within any group or organisation, you can use this to improve your image to other members of that group or organisation. This can have the side effect of making competitors within the group mistrust you and work harder to defeat you, and so requires caution. But if you believe you will benefit from having a stronger image, where people see you as competent and skilful, this is the image you can put across. The power is most often used in a business or the workplace, but does not need to be limited to that and can be used creatively in many organisations and groups.

Attract admiration. This power can be used to make anybody admire you, but works with the most subtle and excellent power when used to influence somebody of superior standing. This might mean somebody of higher social status or somebody who is higher up in an organisation. When directed at such a person, they will come to admire you almost with disregard for your actual talents and actions.

Deserved recognition. If you believe you have worked hard and are not being rewarded for your efforts, this will make the gatekeepers to your success see how good you are, and will fill them with the urge to reward you.

The Sigil of Orobas

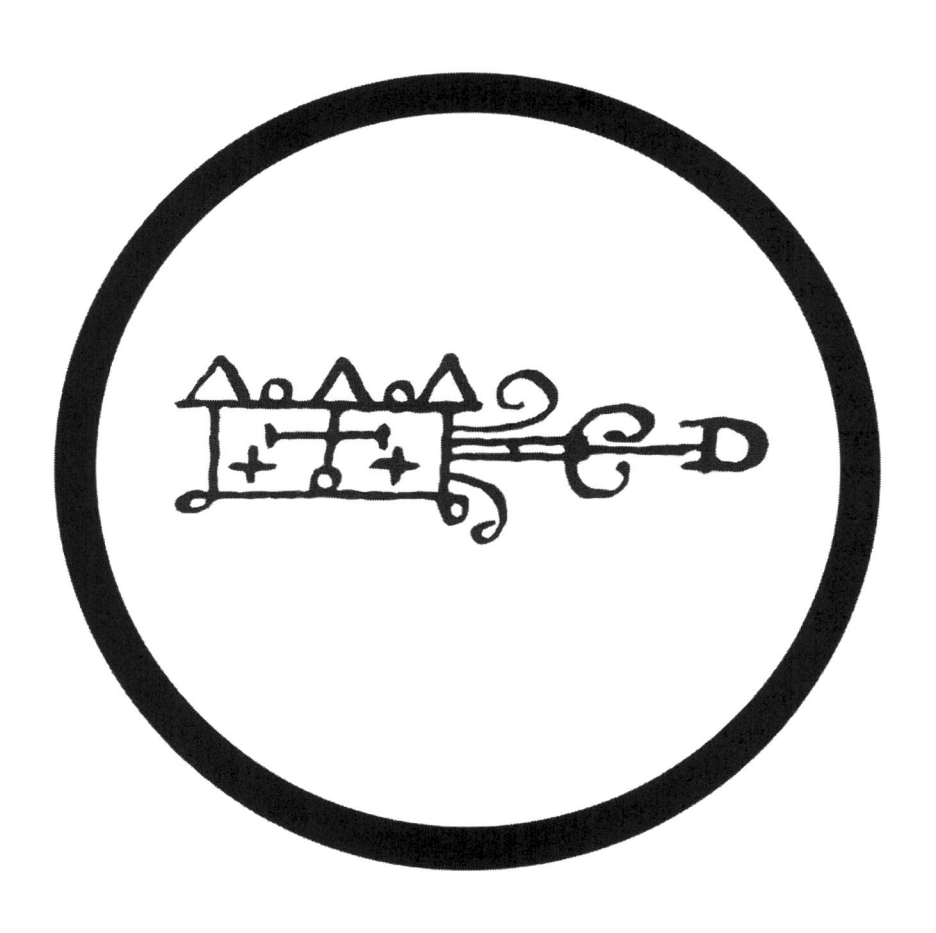

Black cloth stained with white bodily fluids.
The sound of metal being hammered.
The smell of burnt hair.
From a grey darkness grows a dim white light.

56. Gremori

Discover hidden money. If you suspect that somebody is hiding money from you, this power can reveal the truth. This power sounds unimportant because it seems unlikely that anybody would hide money from you. But when you suspect that somebody is dishonest with money in a relationship of any kind – and this happens in business and in romantic relationships – you will find the truth becomes clear to you.

To encourage forbidden attraction. If you are attracted to somebody who is already in a relationship, this power can encourage them to burn with desire for you. It does not create fake feelings, so only works if there is the potential for attraction. When there is, it turns that mild attraction into a burning, lustful desire. Whether or not they act on it is down to your actions and their decisions.

The Sigil of Gremori

A silhouetted bull against the blue twilight.
The sound of wind rushing through bare trees.
The smell of burning wood.
A pale yellow sunset with a crescent moon.

57. Oso

Spiritual exploration. This power shows how wrong people are when they believe demons are only involved with quick, material results. If you are looking to explore spirituality, in whatever way that means to you, you can improve the deep comprehension that comes when you seek spiritual answers. This isn't a power that responds to mere curiosity, but it responds with spectacular results when you are undergoing a spiritual crisis, major life change, or when you need answers to the bigger questions in life. When you feel empty, or when you are seeking to understand your place in reality, and whether you have a method for exploring spirituality or not, let this power guide you. Be open to discovering new ways of exploring your spiritual self, as well as receiving answers and guidance immediately.

Belief in yourself. Even the most positive person can go through periods of self-doubt. You may doubt your abilities or even your worth as a person. When you need to believe in yourself again, this power will bring you a sense of your true value.

An aura of ability. When trying to convince others that you are good at what you do, this power creates an exaggerated perception in others. It doesn't need to be directed at a single person, group, or company (although it can be), but can be used to make your ability in any area appear more impressive and accomplished than it actually is. This is a form of glamour magick which leads you open to discovery if you don't live up to expectations, but used with caution it can be a form of breakthrough magick.

The Sigil of Oso

A dead tree covered with green ivy.
The sound of wind rushing through bare trees.
The smell of rain on grass.
A pale blue sky darkens to a deep blue.

58. Auns

Improve writing. If you write, you can improve your writing and make it feel more valuable to your readers. This power works for any form of writing, but it works best when some flair and creativity is required of you.

Time your actions perfectly. When you are trying to decide the right moment to act, use this power to obtain clarity. You might be looking at the right time to propose marriage, to submit a business proposal, or to make any other request of somebody. Knowing when to act requires skill, but also intuition. Use this magick to obtain insights, intuition, and the calm skill to judge the perfect time to act. This works for any upcoming situation that is important to you.

The Sigil of Auns

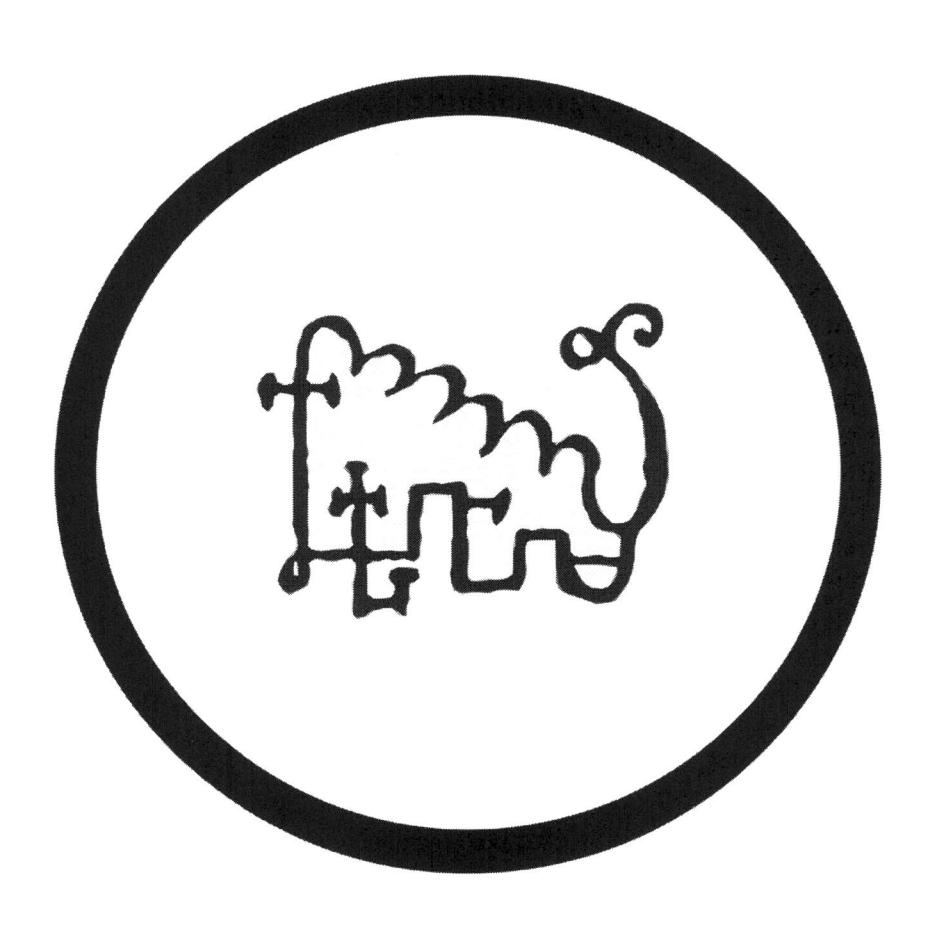

A young woman bears a sword on outstretched palms.
The sound of many people breathing in sleep.
The scent of a distant storm.
A pale yellow sun in a pale blue sky.

59. Orias

Make a neighbour silent. If you have a habitually noisy neighbour, you can use this power to bring stillness and quiet to that household. It won't force somebody to leave but will make them quiet.

Persuade judges. In any form of competition, you can make the judges see you as the worthiest of the big prize. This won't work if you are useless, but if you stand a chance, it will improve your chances of winning or placing well. It's not for competitions like lotteries or gambling but is for skill-based competitions.

Obtain assistance. Use this power to find the right person to assist you in something you wish to achieve. If you know who you want assistance from it can be used to influence them to agree to help.

Change inner thoughts. Using this power, you can make a person change their mind about something. It can be used to win an argument or to obtain something you desire from that person.

The Sigil of Orias

A chalky human skull on a slab of black rock.
The sound of many hissing snakes.
The smell of tart fruit, like berries.
Black clouds touched by amber light.

60. Vapula

Expertise in arts and crafts. When you plan to work on developing your skills in arts or crafts, your efforts will be greatly empowered by this magick. The power improves skills, not creativity, but you will find that when your skills are sharpened, it is easier to be creative.

Develop work skills. Whether you work with your hands or with code, your skills can be improved through magick. This power is most effective when you are setting out to improve an area of your work through study or experimentation.

Pass exams. The power won't make you pass an exam if you don't do the work, but it will mean that any work you put into your study will sink in and be understood. If you want to pass an exam use this power to improve your ability to learn.

The Sigil of Vapula

Rotten leaves surround a black stone.
The angry barking of many dogs.
The scent of animal fur.
A white sky becomes dark with rainclouds.

61. Zagan

Stop a gossip. This works even if you aren't sure who's spreading the gossip.

Subdue a loud or obnoxious person. This can be used at work, on neighbours, or even when somebody close to you is annoying. It's best if you know their name, but if not, you can think about the person (such as an unseen noisy neighbour), and that is often enough.

Make somebody seek forgiveness. When you think somebody has wrong you, this will make them see what they have done and seek to make amends.

For making good investments. If you are fortunate enough to have some spare money to invest, this will help you make good decisions about how to invest, or how to find the right advisors to help.

To become convincing around money. When seeking a financial decision in your favour, this power can help. It is often described as giving you wit, but I think that's misleading. It's more likely to make you seem calm, charming, and convincing than witty.

To improve the productivity of those who work for you. If you have employees, and you need more from them, use this to bring out their natural passion and loyalty. This is not about exploiting workers and making them work harder for less, but about making them a stronger part of your team.

The Sigil of Zagan

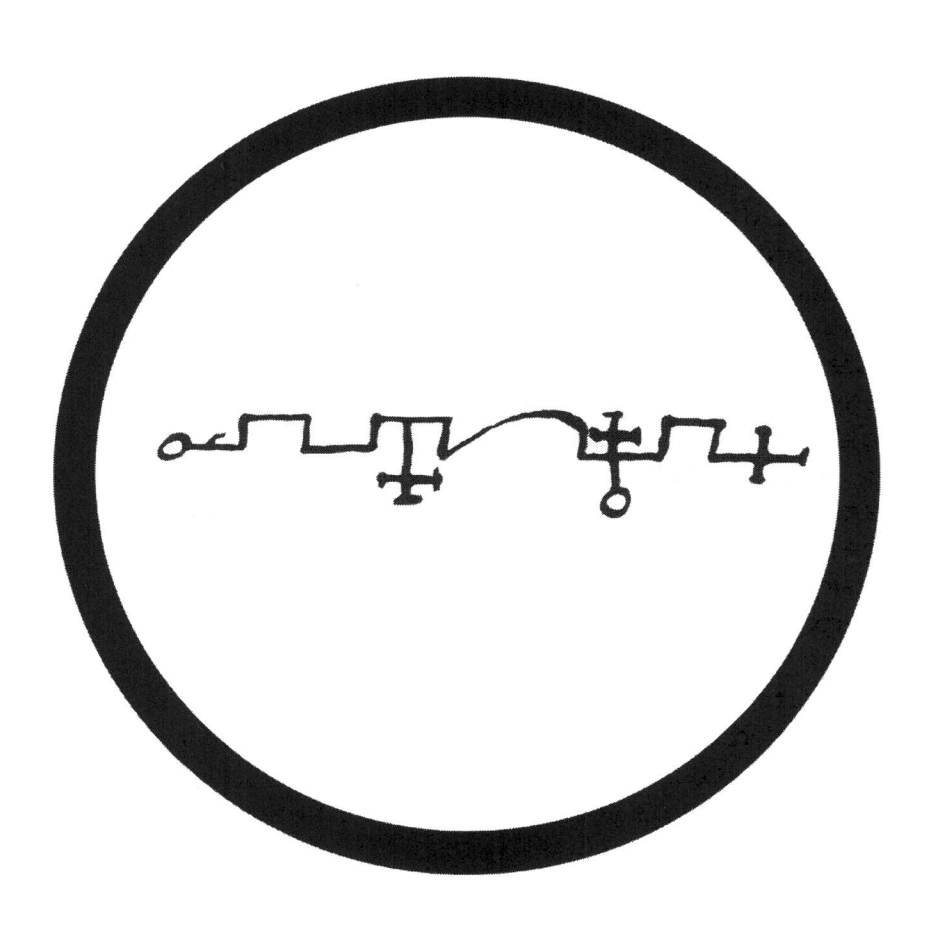

Three dead silvery fish in the grass.
The angry barking of many dogs.
The taste of smoke.
A white sky darkens to black.

62. Valac

Inspired financial wisdom. If you are looking for ideas that could bring money, this power can help you become aware of those ideas. In the days after the ritual, give yourself empty time to daydream or meditate, so that the ideas can break through to consciousness. If you are looking for a few quick ideas for making money, that can work, but the power can also be used when you are seeking a path that will change your main source of income to one that is more productive.

Money from nowhere. A power that sounds as good as this is tempting, but don't let it become your main source of magickal finance, because although it's more reliable than gambling, it's not a way to generate stable income. When you ask for money to come from you in any way that it can, money will come to you, but it is usually anything from a few dollars here and there, to a few hundred dollars. It's not a way to make a living, and although it can work when you really need it to, this power works best when it's more like a game.

Discover betrayal. When you suspect somebody close to you is working against your best interests, this power will cause the truth to come out. You don't direct this at a particular suspect, but ask that any who work in secret against you will be revealed. Used most often to discover traitors in business you should know that it can lead to you discovering affairs and other betrayals.

The Sigil of Valac

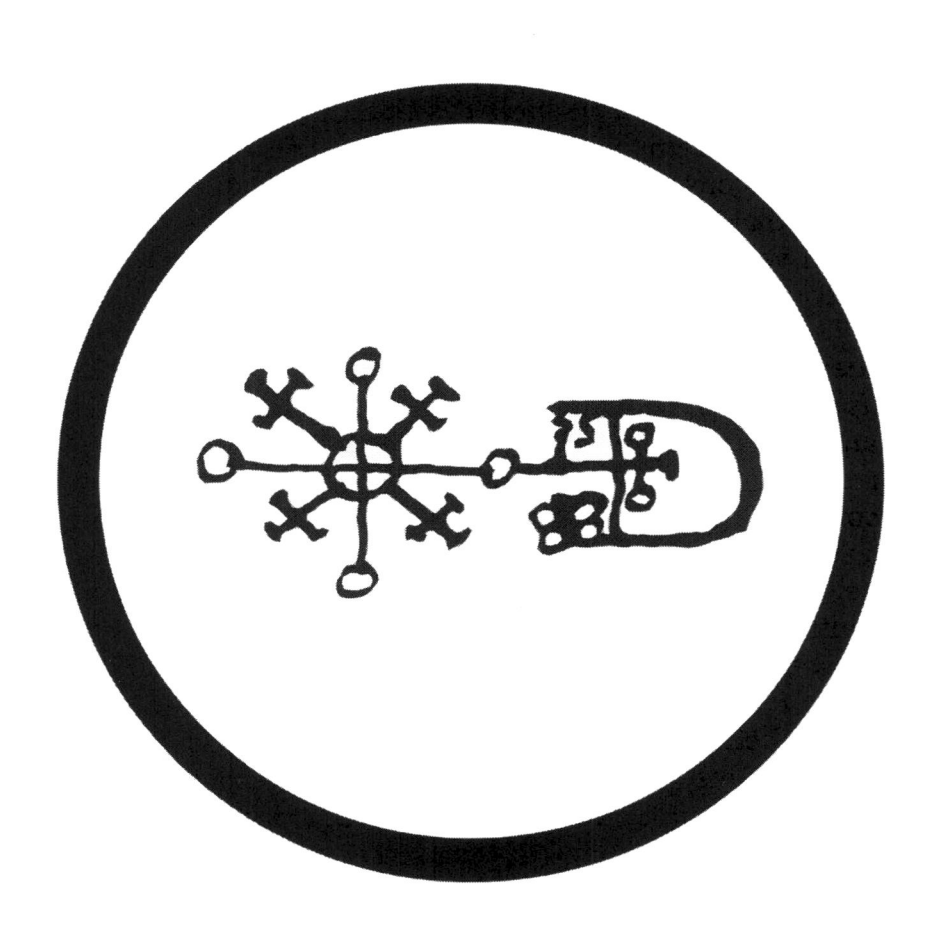

A waterfall breaks on black rocks.
The sound of laboured breathing.
The smell of a stagnant pond.
From a silvery darkness grows glaring white light.

63. Andras

Spread mistrust. With this power, you can make everybody within an organization mistrustful of one another. This causes great disruption. Do not use this when you belong to that organisation, or you too will be mistrusted.

Create fear of a leader. The power will make followers of a leader suffer from a sense of unease and mistrust. It's more likely to work when there's a personal connection, where you know at least one member of the group, or even if you are a member of that group. The power makes people suspicious and lose faith in the one they have trusted. I have seen this bring down several 'leaders' who believed they were untouchable.

Overpower an opposing group. When you are engaged in conflict with another group of people, this power will make your group victorious. It works when there is malice, but can also be effective for overpowering a company you are in competition with. This empowers your group, not just you as an individual. Nobody else in your group needs to know about your magickal efforts.

Generate conflict. Use this power for creating conflict between two people known to you. You will need to know their names. First names will be enough to get a result, but full names are better. The extent of the conflict is not driven by the magick itself, but by the weakness and anger that are already within their relationship. It applies at work as much as it does in romance. It won't always break a relationship, but it can do.

The Sigil of Andras

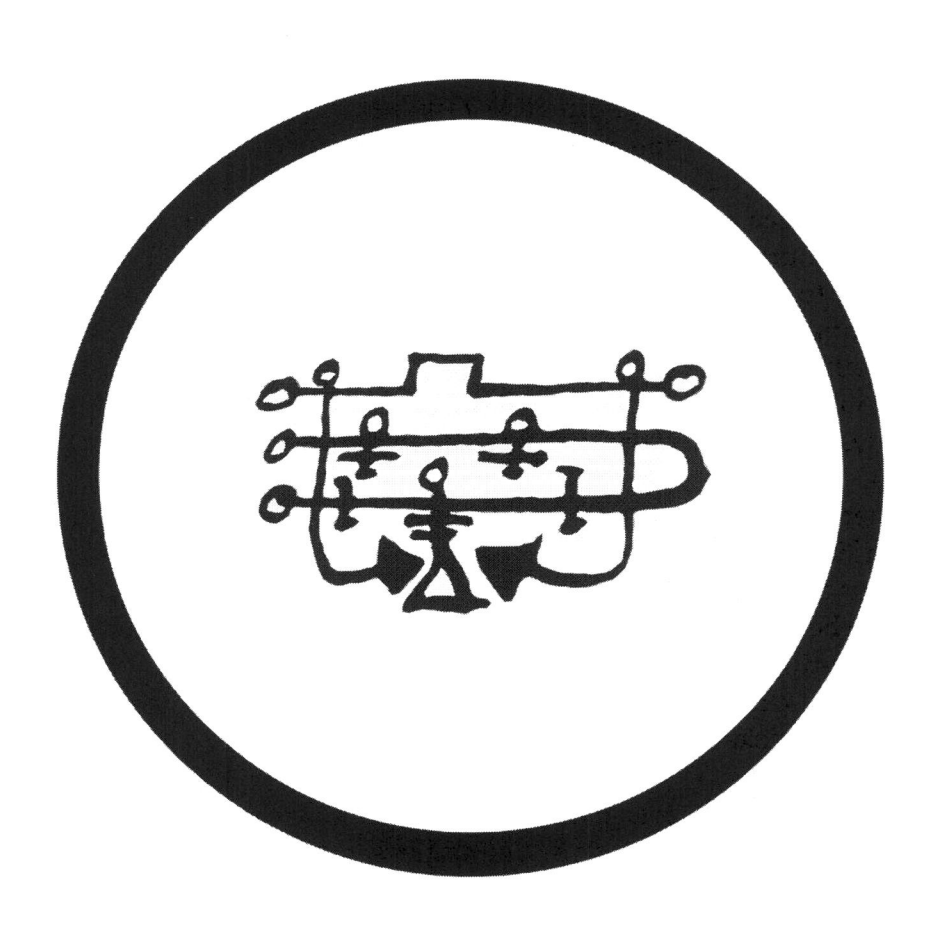

A pile of cold embers.
Birdsong.
The taste of blood.
Blue-grey clouds touched by golden light.

64. Haures

To receive answers. Seek clarity on any issue, from the past, present or future, and an answer should become clear. It will sometimes come in the form of immediate knowledge or intuition, but it may come in the form of growing awareness, or omens that hint at the truth. It is most satisfying when you get the answer during the ritual, or in the time that follows, so if you're the sort of person who can sit in stillness while expecting nothing, do that for half an hour and you might get an answer. If you can't do that, let it come to you at any other time.

Inner justice. When you believe somebody deserves to suffer for something they have done, this power can make them anxious, sad, and confused. The extent of this inner suffering can be extreme, but will be aligned with the level of justice you feel they deserve.

Take success from a business. This is a power that rarely acts quickly, and will not always destroy the business it is aimed at, but it will always create damage in creative ways. The smaller the business, the more rapidly it works. It works most effectively when you have an emotional investment. If the business owner is a competitor or enemy, it will work better than if you dislike the business for more political reasons.

A stream of accidents and poor health. Have you ever met somebody who seems cursed to have one accident or sickness after another? This curse will put somebody in that cycle of misfortune, causing weakness and suffering.

The Sigil of Haures

Black thorns sparkling with droplets of water.
The sound of many hissing snakes.
The taste of charcoal.
A pale yellow sun over a dark ocean.

65. Andrealphus

Urge a confession. When you believe that somebody close to you has lied, or withheld important information that should be shared, you want a confession. This ritual can make people confess their darkest secrets, or secrets that can harm or upset you, so be certain you want to know the truth.

Dream recall and lucidity. The power of Andrealphus makes it possible to become more aware of your dreams upon waking, and even while they occur. If you seek to improve dream recall, to read omens from dreams, or if you are working towards achieving lucidity in a dream, this power can improve your ability to recall dreams clearly.

Clarify the science of connections. If you work in science, architecture, or any other area where connections are important, this power can be used to clarify and even inspire your thoughts. If this sounds abstract to you, it probably doesn't apply, but if you know that you work with the science of connections (and that can even apply in marketing or in the arts) then you can improve your understanding of those connections with this power.

Applied memory. There are many rituals to improve memory, but this power is for when you need to retain knowledge for a practical application. It's often said to be used by doctors and surgeons, but it could also be used by somebody working in the military, or even somebody learning an intricate process for operating machinery. When you need to recall information, with understanding, use this power when you are learning that information to improve your ability to recall it and apply it accurately.

The Sigil of Andrealphus

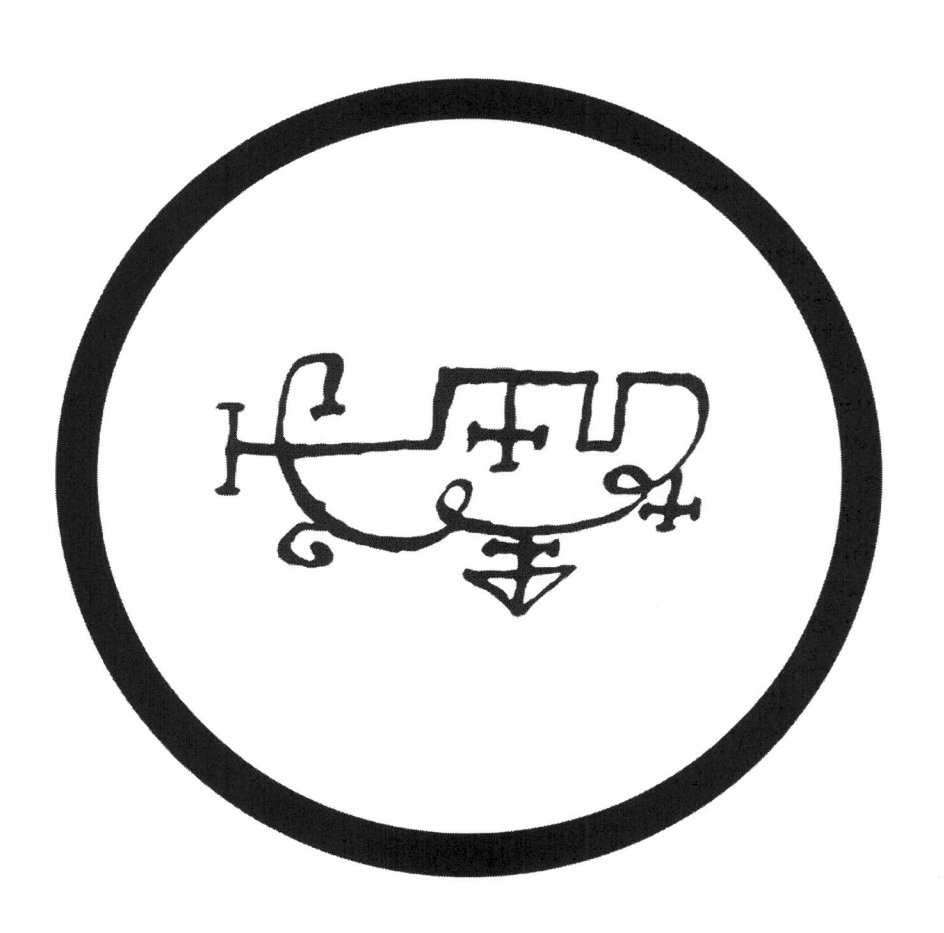

A leaf skeleton on a white marble plinth.
The sound of a cloak falling to the ground.
The smell of crushed leaves.
A pale blue sky brightens to a white glare.

66. Cimeries

Find a lost object. This can work when something has been stolen, but is most likely to help you find something that was lost, whether it's of personal or financial value.

Project Authority. Your aura can be made to seem strong and commanding, so that you project authority. When people see you as a person in authority, they look up to you, they listen to you, and they try to make things go your way. This is invaluable in relationships and business.

Clear out your fears. Inner fears, the ones you aren't really aware of, can dampen your efforts to do well. You may sense that you have such inner fears, and even if you can't sense them, most people have them. It's difficult to find the enthusiasm to perform a ritual to remove inner fears, but if you do you will find an increase in personal strength, productivity, communication, and many other areas that are important for success.

The Sigil of Cimeries

A white rosebud, charred at the edges.
A low humming close to your head.
The scent of a rose.
The blue sky of twilight with a bright full moon.

67. Amducias

Break the will of another. Use against a competitor or enemy, to make them lose the will to compete, continue to fight you, or in any other way that pleases you.

Make somebody compliant. When somebody is resistant to your suggestions, use this power to make them so submissive they are willing to agree with you obediently.

Improve musical ability. For composers, performers, or hobby musicians, this makes it easier to learn and perform. It can help you break bad habits, learn new skills, and perform with flair.

The Sigil of Amducias

The silhouette of a young man before a red morning sun.
Distant thunder.
The smell of freshly dug soil.
A dark night sky with a golden sun.

68. Belial

Bring wealth. I have never found Belial to bring overnight riches, and the power is most effective when you are working on long-term wealth and seek ongoing, stable increases. Call once a month to increase your wealth, and you will find guidance, fortune, and a reward for your efforts, that all increase your wealth.

Discard the unwanted. A power that is easy to underestimate, especially when offered on the same page as riches, the ability to discard an aspect of your life is possibly one of the best in the book. You can choose to discard an attitude, a personality trait, an infatuation, or even situations such as relationships, by asking Belial to remove them from your life.

Become powerful in an organisation. When you need to be more powerful in an organisation, you need to progress in a way that is stealthy when required but also to be seen, respected, and desired by those who could let you obtain power. With a simple request, Belial can aid your real-world efforts. Even though it may take months to get where you are going, the benefits begin soon after the ritual.

Win political favour. Whether you are dealing with office arguments, personal battles that involve several people, or actual politics, this power can make you win the favour of others. In any situation where political-style sides are being taken, and you wish to be seen as a leader, a worthy advisor, or somebody who can be trusted, this power will make others favour you above all others.

Emanate power. This power is not directed at anybody else, but at transforming your aura so that you project an awe-inspiring sense of power. Other people will come to see you as somebody to be respected.

The Sigil of Belial

Rocks covered with wet moss.
The sound of many people breathing in sleep.
The taste of honey.
A pale green sky with a golden sun.

69. Decarabia

Good speaking skills. When you're speaking to groups as small as a minor workforce, or making a major speech, this power can give you the ability to be spontaneous and impactful.

Disguise your activities and plans. Make any investigation into you, whether amateur and casual, or serious and professional, be concealed by a fog of misperception. This helps you to make and implement plans without being caught. You can protect a situation, hiding it from any and all who might investigate. A second way to use this to make a named person (such as a boss, lover, or friend) unable to see what you are doing.

The Sigil of Decarabia

Ashes at the base of a dead tree.
Birdsong.
The scent of animal fur.
A deep blue sky fades to black.

70. Seer

Manipulate time. This power will give you the ability to get more done when time is pressing. It doesn't make you more efficient or determined, but seems to curve and alter your personal experience of time so that you are able to do more. You can direct this at life in general, but that makes its power quite weak. The strongest effect is found when you have an urgent project that needs to be finished in a short space of time, such as a few hours, days, or weeks.

Get the decision you want. When you're waiting for a decision from somebody else, even if it's a group of people, bring this power to bear on the decision. It will be made swiftly and will be aligned with what you desire.

Solve a personal problem with great speed. When you have an issue with another person, this power can bring about a solution rapidly. It doesn't always mean you will get precisely what you want, but it means the problematic situation will be resolved. It works well on those annoying situations that you want to get out of your life, by reducing the willpower and interest of the person who's unsettling you.

The Sigil of Seer

An old man bears a sword on outstretched palms.
The sound of a cloak falling to the ground.
The scent of a storm.
White lightning in a clear blue sky.

71. Dantalion

Project charisma. This power gives you an easy charm that makes people want to be near you.

To attract potential lovers into your life. If you have any social life, you will find yourself meeting more potential lovers during the following months. This does nothing to make you more attractive, but you should obtain more opportunities for love. You will also have more awareness of when you have an opportunity.

Know the mind of another. Gain insights into another person when you interact with them (through deeper perception), or when you focus on them in your mind (through intuition and insights).

Influence feelings. Direct this at anybody you know personally, and you can shift their feelings. You can use this as a weapon to make somebody feel shame, doubt, or misery, or you can use it to lift somebody's mood. It can be used to influence romantic feelings, but only works if there are some feelings there to begin with.

To assist with any sincere concern or desire. Many people come to rely on Dantalion more than any other spirit, because for any concern you can be given wisdom, fortune, and the ability to change inner and outer reality according to your desire. Should you throw the rest of the book out? I don't believe so, as every demon has qualities and powers you will treasure, but never dismiss the power of Dantalion.

The Sigil of Dantalion

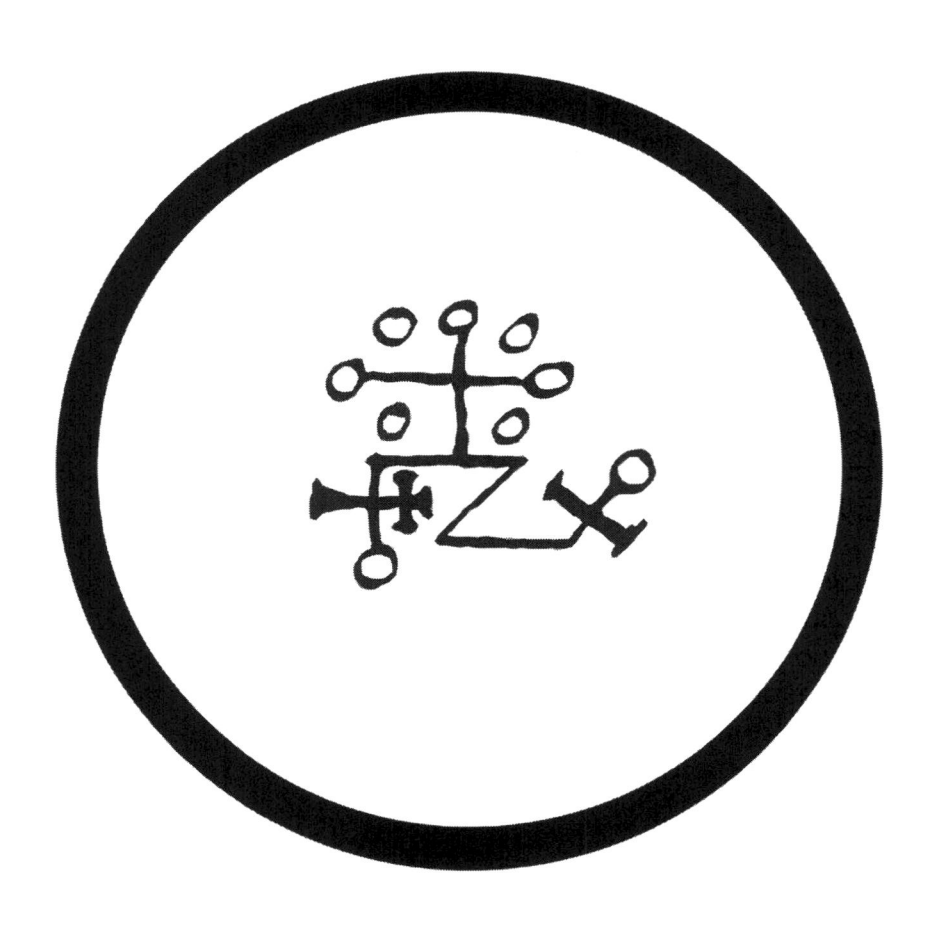

A wall of brass, shimmering in candle light.
A low humming close to your head.
The smell of burnt hair.
A yellow sky warms to amber as a scarlet sun rises.

72. Andromalius

Create unease. This will make somebody uneasy, yet functional, which can make them easier to manipulate. It can also be used as a mild punishment. It should be used on somebody you have met in person for the best results.

Bring an end to extortion, blackmail, or any threat. This works whether the threats are real, bluster, public, or private.

Make the hated fear you. This can be used at any time, to make a hated person fear you.

Make a disloyal person reveal the truth. You can use this at home or work, and direct it at a person that you suspect of disloyalty. If nothing is revealed within two or three weeks, by accident, discovery, or confession, you can trust that there is loyalty.

Discover a subtle thief who continually takes from you. This is ideal when you know somebody has been stealing from you, but you have not worked out who the culprit might be. You might catch them, work it out, or make them slip up.

Gain insight into an ambition. When you have a goal, mission, or another project, use magick to see if you need to pursue this course of action. It's a good way to drop goals that won't bring you happiness or fulfilment, and commit to goals that will.

The Sigil of Andromalius

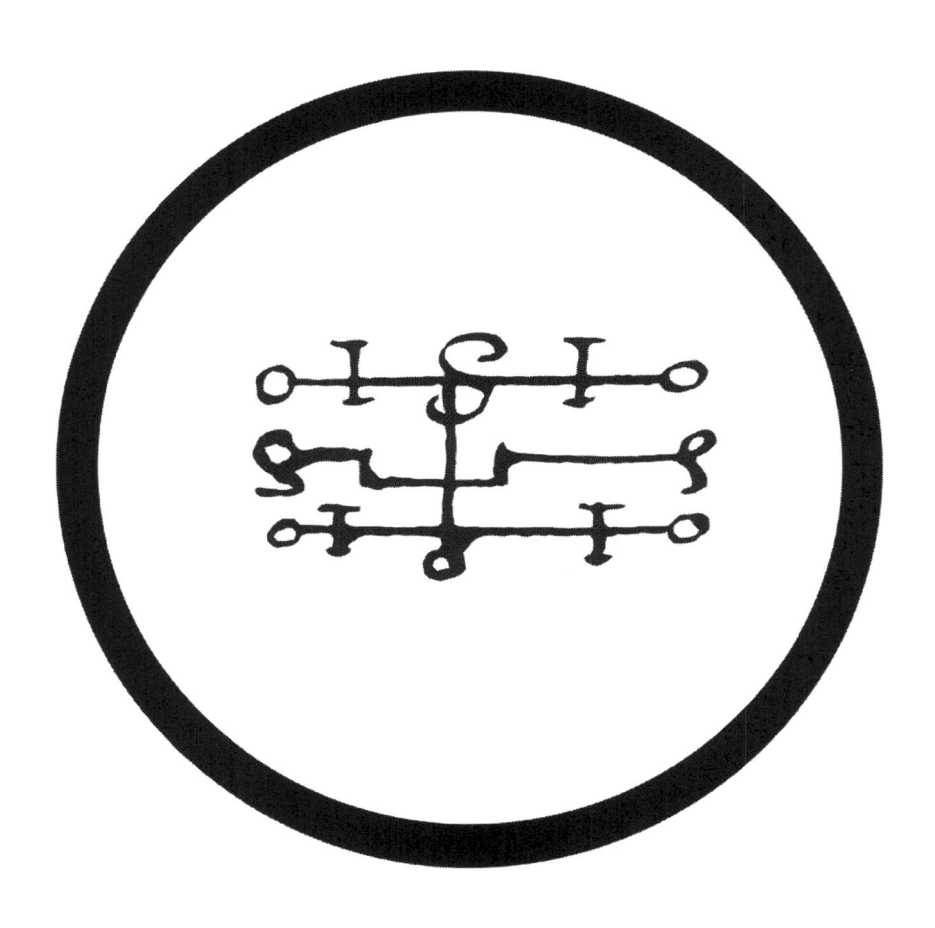

A broken black boulder on chalky soil.
The sound of lustful moaning, as from a drowsy orgy.
A smell like wet straw.
The black sky becomes grey with clouds.

Questions and Answers

Q: I have a really bad imagination. I can't imagine anything. Can I still use this magick?

A: Yes. Read the early chapters again. It's not about visualization. If you want, you can read the pathworkings without attempting to picture anything.

Q: Can I speak the names, words, and images out loud?

A: If it helps you, yes, you can do anything, but I suggest trying to perform the ritual silently. In silence, your focus on breath and imagery is more powerful than when you're making noise.

Q: Can I breathe onto the sigil in the book, or do I need to make a new copy?

A: Use the one in the book, even if it's the eBook. The imagery is there in front of you and will work.

Q: Can I use powers for these demons that are listed by other authors?

A: I said earlier that you can, but I think it's worth saying that some authors and experimenters have gone way over the top, suggesting that certain demons have all these weird powers, and a lot of it is invented crap. I've also said that demons have powers that are not always widely known, and that you may discover these when you work with a demon. You might get an instinct. The thing with these powers is that they can work for you, but might not for everybody. Try anything you want, but the powers most likely to work are the ones described here. This book isn't meant to be something you try out for the hell of it. I hope you'll be using it twenty years from now. By then you'll know how to get the most out of any demon you care to summon.

Q: Can I do more than one ritual in a day? I've spent three days getting ready, so it seems like a waste not to make the most of the time.

A: Do you need to? This book deals with wants and lusty desires, so you don't have to aspire only for your highest needs. But most magick fails because of impatience. How long has it taken you to find magick, or this book? Can you wait a few more days? One ritual each day is the most I'd recommend.

Q: When I've summoned a demon with the pathworking, can I make several requests?

A: Same answer as above. Can't it wait?

Q: Can I use the magick on other people?

A: Many of the rituals are aimed at influencing other people, which means by extension that you can try to help other people or direct powers at them. The effects are not as predictable as when you use magick for your own needs, because people are the way they are for many reasons, and if you try to force change on them with magick, they might resist the change for the sake of comfort.

Q: Can I influence people I don't know?

A: Knowing the person in the real world, even casually, is the strongest connection there is, so try to work magick on people you have met. But what if you want to curse an unknown stranger who robbed your house? You can. You tell the demon who you mean, and that will be enough.

Q: Can I levitate, change my eye colour, meet a celebrity, or become a god?

A: I doubt it. Magick is powerful but not ridiculous. When used as a fantasy, it's wasted effort. Use magick as a way to change yourself and your reality, without getting carried away by some of the crazy stuff people like to waste time pretending is real.

Q: Why are there no god names or angels? I don't feel safe.

A: Don't panic just because this is different. If you want to make all the usual divine calls and speak every angelic name you know, try that and see if it helps or hinders. Or try what's described for pathworking because that's what this book is about, and I wouldn't write about it if I thought it was risky.

Q: Some powers sound really similar to each other. Which should I use?

A: Work with a demon who has other powers that you find appealing, or that are vaguely related to your request. And read carefully, because some powers that sound the same have subtle differences.

Q: This seems complicated. Isn't there a way to make this easier?

A: If you want to try a simple spell, write down your wish, throw it in a fire, and forget about it. That's simple folk magick, and lots of people believe in it. *This* book's magick summons demons in a way that is so simple, it would have been undreamt of by many occultists of old. This is magick that happens almost automatically by reading the instructions and following them. The problem with modern magick is that it's so simple it seems like a basic spell, and when it seems that simple, it's tempting to ask for it to be even easier. It can't get much easier. Skip steps and change things if you want, but it might not work.

Q: Why is the Water element for Ronove a sound when it should be a taste or scent?

A: Here, the sound of Birdsong represents the element of Water. Theoretically, I think this suggests that Birdsong is sufficiently representative of whatever elemental state the demon requires. It would be tidier to have a different image to this, but what matters is that it works this way.

Q: How often should I repeat a ritual?

A: The ritual only needs to be performed once. If you think you stuffed it up, you're probably being too hard on yourself (unless you didn't read the instructions properly). If you think you stuffed up, do it again, but don't try to be perfect. Some rituals mention repetition after a certain time or when things have changed. Otherwise, once is enough.

Q: Should I repeat a ritual if it didn't work?

A: I'll repeat something from earlier. *You should expect results but don't go into a sulk when something doesn't work first time. A small failure is usually a step to a bigger success. If you don't panic.* And I'll add to that by saying that that old cliché of 'letting go' really works. If you struggle and hope and worry, you're forcefully believing in the problem, the lack. If you let go and forget about the result you want, as though it will happen, it probably will.

Q: Can I use this to evoke demons?

A: It's not designed for that. If you're using another evocation technique and want to slot pathworking in there, I bet it will help you make the connection, but by itself, it's not going to get you to evocation. You will get a result, and you will feel The Summoned Presence, so the supernatural reality of the magick will be there. I know some people really want to feel the reality of the demons before they believe magick will work. You don't need to feel anything, but The Summoned Presence will be felt by many readers, especially if you work with this over several months and get used to the magick. I think you should try to develop trust without needing to feel the presence of the demon, but I also know you might not expect much and then be quite surprised at how strong a sense of demonic presence you feel. Awe is not fear, and you can remain confident that any demon you sense has been called in a way that means it's waiting for your desire and is willing to cooperate with you.

Q: Is there one thing I can do to make it more likely to work?

A: *Trust* and *sincerity* are words that many other authors have used, and I will use them in this answer. You don't have to force belief, but you'll get more out of the magick if you have something you really want and hand your desire to the demon, trusting that the result will come. If you test the magick, to see if it's up to your lofty standards, that's the wrong approach. Sincerity doesn't mean purity. You can sincerely want to have sex or curse somebody.

Q: Are the spirits real or egregores?

A: If you don't know what an egregore is, it's a sort of invented spirit that's come about by accident or design. Sometimes, if people perform a fake ritual for long enough, it sort of works, by connecting you to something like the spirit, a thoughtform copy of the spirit, or a part of the spirit. There's a lot of fear these days that some magick connects you only to egregors of the *Goetia* demons. It's a reasonable fear because some really crap magick has been published. I can't boast about how genuine these demons are, but to answer the question, I believe the spirits are real and that they are not egregores. Your own experience of the rituals and the results will answer this for you.

Q: Can I combine this with other methods, like your Magickal Influence method?

A: If you try adding this to somebody else's magick, as an extra push to get it to work, you might get a brilliant result, but it might make no difference. Experiment if that's your thing.

In *Magickal Influence* I used a method that involved calling on angels and drawing the sigil. Some people loved that method and will be pissed that I didn't write a whole book using that method. If you liked it enough, you can use the names, sigils, and powers in this book with that method. What's not included in this book are the angelic names you need, but you can find them elsewhere. There are different versions in many books, but you'll find names that work in Jacobus Swart's *The Book of Immediate Magick Part 1* or Gordon Winterfield' *Demons of Magick*. Using *this* book, one of those books, with *Magickal Influence*, you can put together a system that works. Why don't I provide my version of the names in this book? It would make this book too complicated and confused and would make people think they *had* to use that method. That's not what this book is about. The method in *Magickal Influence* is a good one, which is why I put it in that book, but I prefer pathworking, so if you want to use all the powers my recommendation is to use the method the way I've set it out here. If you want to mix other things in, like those angel names, you can see what happens. It might work really well for you. But be aware that in *Magickal Influence* I didn't always use the standard correspondences. For each of the seventy-two angels, there's a set of names that supposedly correspond to one demon. That's the theory. But I found that sometimes, switching the angels around provides a better result for certain situations. This is another reason I've not included all that here. It would take a long book to show all the variations and combinations that I've found to be useful.

Instead, you get pathworking, which works without the need for the rest of it.

If you're really attached to the method from *Magickal Influence*, use it if you want, but remember I shared that method because it was simple enough and good enough for influence. This book makes all the powers of the demons available, and pathworking is my recommended method for getting to those powers.

Alternative Names

The demon names used in this book are the ones I know best, and the ones I believe are most likely to work. If you don't connect with the name, here are the known alternatives for each demon.

1. Bael is also known as Baell and Baëll.

2. Agares is primarily known as Agares.

3. Vassago is also known as Vasago.

4. Gamigin is also known as Gamygyn and Samigina

5. Marbas is also known as Barbas

6. Valefar is also known as Valefor, Malaphar, and Malephar.

7. Amon is also known as Aamon.

8. Barbatos is primarily known as Barbatos.

9. Paimon is primarily known as Paimon.

10. Buer is primarily known as Buer.

11. Gusoin is primarily known as Gusoin.

12. Sitri is also known as Sytry and Bitru.

13. Beleth is also known as Byleth and Bileth.

14. Leraye is also known as Laraie, Leraje, Leraic, Leraikha, Loray, and Oray.

15. Eligos is also known as Eligor and Abigor

16. Zepar is primarily known as Zepar.

17. Botis is also known as Otis.

18. Bathin is also known as Marthim.

19. Sallos is also known as Saleos and Zaleos.

20. Purson is also known as Pursan and Curson.

21. Marax is also known as Morax and Foraii.

22. Ipos is also known as Ipes, Ayperos, and Ayporos

23. Aim is also known as Aym, Haborym, and Haborim

24. Naberius is also known as Naberus and Cerberus

25. Glasya Labolas is also known as Glasya-la bolas, Caacrinolaas, and Caassimolar.

26. Bime is also known Bimé, Bune and Bim.

27. Ronove is also known as Ronové and Roneve.

28. Berith is also known as Beall, Berithi, and Bolfri.

29. Astaroth is primarily known as Astaroth.

30. Forneus is also known as Forners.

31. Foras is also known as Forcas and Forras.

32. Asmodai is also known as Asmoday, Sidonai, and Sydonay.

33. Gaap is also known as Gäap and Tap.

34. Furfur is also known as Furtur.

35. **Marchosias** is also known as Marchocias.

36. **Stolas** is also known as Stolus and Stolos.

37. **Phenix** is also known as Phoenix, Phenex, and Pheynix.

38. **Halphas** is primarily known as Halphas.

39. **Malphas** is primarily known as Malphas.

40. **Raum** is also known as Raim and Räum.

41. **Forcalor** is also known as Focalor, Focator, and Furcalor.

42. **Vepar** is also known as Vephar and Separ.

43. **Sabnock** is also known as Sabnac, Salmac, Sabnack, Sabnach, and Savnok.

44. **Shax** is also known as Chax and Scox.

45. **Vine** is also known as Viné and Vinea.

46. **Bifrons** is also known as Bifrovs, Bifrous, and Bifröus.

47. **Vuall** is also known as Wal, Vual, Uvall, and Voval.

48. **Haagenti** is primarily known as Haagenti.

49. **Crocell** is also known as Crokel, Procel, and Procell.

50. **Furcas** is primarily known as Furcas.

51. **Balam** is also known as Balaam.

52. **Alloces** is also known as Allocer, Alocer, and Alocas.

53. **Caim** is also known as Cäim, Caym, and Camio.

54. **Murmus** is also known as Murmur and Murmux.

55. **Orobas** is also known as Obus.

56. **Gremori** is also known as Gemory, Gremory, Gamori and Gomory.

57. **Oso** is also known as Ose, Osé, Oze, and Voso.

58. **Auns** is also known as Amy and Avnas.

59. **Orias** is also known as Oriax.

60. **Vapula** is also known as Naphula, Nappula, and Valpula.

61. **Zagan** is also known as Zagam.

62. **Valac** is also known as Valu, Volac, and Ualac.

63. **Andras** is primarily known as Andras.

64. **Haures** is also known as Flauros, Hauros, and Hauras.

65. **Andrealphus** is also known as Androalphus.

66. **Cimeries** is also known as Cimeies, Cimejes, and Kimaris.

67. **Amducias** is also known as Amduscias, and Amdukias.

68. **Belial** is also known as Beliall.

69. **Decarabia** is also known as Carabia.

70. **Seer** is also known as Seere, Sear, and Seir.

71. **Dantalion** is also known as Dantaylion.

72. **Andromalius** is primarily known as Andromalius.

Unbibliography

Bibliographies are often a way to show off how many books you've read. I'm almost embarrassed to show the number of books I've read that relate to *Goetia* and demons. You don't need a bibliography for me to prove that.

The main ideas in this book were developed by the occult orders I've worked with, fleshed out by my work as a practicing occultist, with many years of testing.

An afternoon of homemade chaos magick can provide results with *Goetia*, but from my experience, there is magick that works, magick that works unpredictably, and magick that can lead to a burdensome misinterpretation. That is, some *Goetia* methods work, some are fanciful crap, and some make things worse.

I can't guarantee that everything in this book will work for you every time, but I can guarantee it won't make things worse or backfire. I can guarantee that you won't be punished or made to suffer if you mess up a ritual. If life gets worse when you use any magick it's usually because magick has been stuck onto the problem too late, so late in the bedlam of your life that it's difficult to get results.

Mostly, if you use the magick as described, and if you avoid entitlement, you'll get what you want. I called this chapter the *Unbibliography*, but I will mention some authors you can read. If you don't know already, the useful historians for *Goetia* are Joseph Peterson, Stephen Skinner, and David Rankine, as a place to start your fact-checking. But if you want to get your hands on the materials used by practicing occultists during the past thirty years, you don't need to do any more research because it's already in this book, and although it's not an academic volume filled with references, it's a gateway to experience. That will teach you more about demons than any author could.

I hope you enjoy the experience of magick. I hope you value this book. Thank you for your support. If you appreciate this book's value, a good review on Amazon makes it easier for me to carry on with what is a time-consuming and expensive hobby. But always be honest when you review. Nobody wants to read false praise. If you like what you've read, let others know, and this magickal current will continue to burn brightly.

Sincerely,

Corwin Hargrove

More from Corwin Hargrove

Practical Jinn Magick
Rituals to Unleash the Powers of
The Fire Spirits

Demons of Wrath
The Dark Fires of Attack Magick

The Demons of Deception
Rituals to Hide the Truth, Create Confusion
and Conceal Your Actions

The Magick of Influence
Persuade, Control and Dominate with
The Forces of Darkness

Printed in Great Britain
by Amazon